THE
ETIOLOGY OF ELDER ABUSE
BY ADULT OFFSPRING

THE
ETIOLOGY OF ELDER ABUSE BY ADULT OFFSPRING

By

GEORGIA J. ANETZBERGER, Ph.D., A.C.S.W.

Consultant/Administrator of Adult Services
Cuyahoga County Department of Human Services

Advisor on Adult Services
Geauga County Department of Human Services

Director for the Project
"Abuse of Elder Parents in the Home"
Case Western Reserve University

Chair, Ohio Coalition for Adult Protective Services

Member, Governor's Task Force on Family Violence

CHARLES C THOMAS · PUBLISHER
Springfield · Illinois · U.S.A.

Published and Distributed Throughout the World by

CHARLES C THOMAS • PUBLISHER

2600 South First Street

Springfield, Illinois 62794-9265

© *1987 by* CHARLES C THOMAS • PUBLISHER

ISBN 0-398-05297-2

Library of Congress Catalog Card Number: 86-23010

With THOMAS BOOKS *careful attention is given to all details of manufacturing and
design. It is the Publisher's desire to present books that are satisfactory as to their physical
qualities and artistic possibilities and appropriate for their particular use.* THOMAS
BOOKS *will be true to those laws of quality that assure a good name and good will.*

Printed in the United States of America

Q-R-3

Library of Congress Cataloging in Publication Data

Anetzberger, Georgia J. (Georgia Jean)
    The etiology of elder abuse by adult offspring.

    Originally presented as the author's thesis (Ph.D.)--
Case Western Reserve University.
    Bibliography: p.
    Includes index.
    1. Aged--United States--Abuse of--Case studies.
2. Adult children--United States--Family relationships--
Case studies. 3. Parents, Aged--United States--Family
relationships--Case studies. I. Title.
HV1461.A67   1987   362.6'042   86-23010
ISBN 0-398-05297-2

DEDICATIONS

IN MEMORY OF Judith Shelley Eldridge, former supervisor at the Summit County Department of Human Services, who pioneered in the provision of sound adult protective services in the State of Ohio.

In celebration of the eightieth birthday of George John Anetzberger, my father, who gives the family a wonderful model for conviction and social responsibility.

PREFACE

ECAUSE elder abuse was only recently recognized as a social problem, there has been little research on its etiology, and none using the perpetrators as subjects of study. Consequently, understanding of the phenomenon has been limited to the perceptions of victims or their service providers, and analogy with other abused populations. In an effort to explain the physical abuse of elderly parents by their adult offspring, exploratory research was conducted in Northeast Ohio using purposive comparison for the research design. Meaningful explanatory variables were systematically identified and examined and their interrelationships explored through two in-depth and focused interviews with a panel of abusing adult offspring. The initial basis for inquiry emphasized existing theoretical perspectives set within a conceptual framework. Interview schedules were specially developed for the study, and included indices to measure social isolation, burden of elder caregiving, social intimacy, and conflict tactics.

Participating hospitals and human service agencies identified 40 adult offspring who qualified for inclusion in the study. Of these, 15 were interviewed, although background information was obtained from referral source caseworkers on the total research sample, and used in demonstrating the interviewed sample to be representative of the whole. Findings portrayed the typical abusing adult offspring as an unmarried, middle-aged man with pathological characteristics. The elder parent he abuses is his natural mother with whom he has lived for several years. He recently inflicted three different forms of violence on her. She is very old and both physically and mentally impaired. The typical abusing adult offspring often provides considerable care to his elder parent. However, he is burdened by her disturbing behaviors and his lack of available time for personal pursuits. He perceives himself socially isolated in the caregiving role, particularly from supportive extended family. Moreover, contrary to popular opinion, he did not grow up in an abusive family.

Further content analysis of responses from the interviewed sample enabled the differentiation of three subject groups, as well as the identification of specific steps triggering abuse occurrence. Implications of the study for social policy and programming as well as further research are also discussed.

ACKNOWLEDGMENTS

EVERY RESEARCHER quickly learns that the successful completion of any investigation depends on the help and support of many other persons. This effort is certainly no exception.

The research was submitted in partial fulfillment of the requirements for the degree of Doctor of Philosophy in social welfare at Case Western Reserve University in Cleveland, Ohio. For this reason, initial gratitude is extended to Thomas Holland, my thesis advisor, who offered the right amounts of guidance, support and independence for me to undertake the study. I also wish to thank the other members of my committee, Claudia Coulton, Ruth Dunkle and Kevin Eckert. Each provided important perspective to the research. I appreciate the time and assistance of every committee member.

Thanks go to Jill Korbin, principal investigator for the National Institute on Aging funded "Abuse of Elder Parents in the Home" project, for her help in constructing the first interview schedule and encouragement during the whole research process.

A research sample would not have been obtained without the cooperation of representatives from the 21 participating hospitals and human service agencies. Many of them gave considerable time to the study, and unfortunately must remain anonymous. However, their interest in elder abuse and steadfast willingness to help identify a sample maintained the study's momentum during some difficult periods of subject identification. In addition, some hospital and agency staff assisted in the development of indices for the interview schedules and one social worker interviewed one of the abusing adult offspring. I will always be grateful for their contributions.

Special appreciation goes to Sally Reisacher, Elizabeth Zborowsky, Susan Wetzler and Phyllis Solomon who made helpful suggestions, including how to make the interview schedules more readable and how to access certain programs on the computer. Thanks also to Carol Miller and Vi Chapman for assisting with some of the typing of manuscript drafts.

My gratitude is extended to the filial caregivers and representatives of Appalachian culture who agreed to be interviewed. Their reflections have helped to deepen our understanding of elder abuse and hopefully will lead to better programs and policies for assisting elderly victims of family violence.

Any understanding that requires a great deal of time and energy is made easier by the personal support of friends and family. In this I have received more than my fair share of the very best available. My most profound appreciation goes to Carol Miller and Anne Wayant, my closest friends, and George Anetzberger and Toni Gukich, my father and sister, for their love, encouragement, patience and interest.

Finally, I wish to thank the many other persons who are not specifically named in these acknowledgments but who contributed to the completion of the study in significant ways.

CONTENTS

THE
ETIOLOGY OF ELDER ABUSE
BY ADULT OFFSPRING

CHAPTER I

BACKGROUND:
EXPLANATIONS OF ELDER ABUSE

PROBLEM RECOGNITION

ELDER ABUSE is the maltreatment of older persons. It includes hitting, shoving and slapping, all of which can cause pain, injury and in some instances even death to the victim.

Elder abuse only recently was recognized as a social problem. Robert Butler, in his 1975 Pulitzer Prize-winning book, *Why Survive? Being Old in America,* acknowledged a "battered old person syndrome." Susan Steinmetz, widely-acclaimed authority on domestic violence, testified in 1978 before a committee of the U.S. House of Representatives on overlooked aspects of family violence. In her testimony she stated:

> *Our knowledge about the battered elderly mirrors our knowledge of the extent of child abuse in the early 60s or the extent of our knowledge about wife abuse in the early 70s. If we were to label the 60s as the decade of interest in child abuse, and the 70s as decade of wife abuse studies, then I predict, given the generally increasing concern for the elderly and more specifically concern of abuse of elderly in public institutions, that the 80s will be the decade of the Battered Parent (Steinmetz, 1978, p. 7).*

There were no journal, newspaper or magazine articles; no papers presented at gerontological and other conferences; and no systematic research specifically on the problem of elder abuse before 1978. Besides Butler, the only evidence of problem recognition before that time comes indirectly from some of the publications on adult protective services (e.g., Blenkner et al, 1971; Horowitz and Estes, 1971). However, since adult protective services traditionally focused more on the frail and impaired and self-neglected elderly than on the abused elderly, even here problem recognition was minimal.

3

Since 1978 there have been numerous articles, many conference papers and several attempts to systematically research the problem. Reasons for recent interest in the problem are many and include the following: (1) The recent attention given to such abused populations as children and women helped to alert the public that another vulnerable population may suffer similarly from their caregivers. (2) The growing attention given to older persons as their proportion of the population increased stimulated interest in all matters affecting their well-being. (3) The probable greater incidence of elder abuse itself helped trigger attention to a growing problem. One likely reason for increased incidence of elder abuse concerns the fact that the largest increases in the elderly population have occurred among the very old and among women (Brody, 1982; Nowak, 1983; U.S. Senate Special Committee on Aging and American Association of Retired Persons, 1984), the very ones thought most likely to experience elder abuse (Lau and Kosberg, 1979; Block and Sinnott, 1979; O'Malley et al, 1979; Steur and Austin, 1980).

Most publications and research on elder abuse have focused on the nature and incidence of the problem. Scant attention has been given to causal explanation. Those explanations that have been offered usually have their origins in the literature on other abused populations, particularly children. Children and elderly persons do have certain characteristics in common, including: (1) vulnerability by virtue of physical and mental underdevelopment in the case of most children and physical or mental impairment in the case of some elders, and (2) economic and social dependency on the part of most children and some elders. However, elders, even impaired elders, are not simply old children. They are different because of their legal status as adults and extensive life experiences, among other factors. Therefore, explanation of elder abuse requires separate consideration. That this has not yet adequately happened reflects the recent recognition given the problem area. Understanding the nature of the problem logically precedes understanding its etiology.

RELEVANCE FOR SOCIAL WELFARE

The present study focuses on elder abuse by adult offspring. It specifically seeks to understand why sons and daughters physically abuse their elderly parents. The locus of the study is on abuse as a problem for elders living in the community, residing in their own homes or the homes of other persons, but not institutionalized in a nursing home or other such setting.

Explaining elder abuse is a theoretical problem of significance for the field of social welfare. The concerns of social welfare are to minimize human suffering and improve social functioning. In both respects, the traditional emphasis is on meeting human needs while maintaining social order (Zald, 1965; Wilensky and Lebeaux, 1974; Gilbert and Specht, 1974). Elder abuse exemplifies human suffering in the physical injury and pain as well as in the mental anguish experienced by the abused elder (Lau and Kosberg, 1979; Rathbone-McCuan, 1980; U.S. House Select Committee on Aging, 1981, 1985). It indicates social malfunctioning in the destructive relations between caregiver and elder that can contribute to abuse and the disjointed relations that can result from abuse occurrence (Steinmetz, 1981). Elder abuse illustrates a failure to meet human needs around personal safety and dignity.

Explaining the etiology of elder abuse furthers an understanding of family dysfunctions and intergenerational family violence. It offers the necessary theoretical framework for establishing appropriate policies and programs for eradicating the problem; it gives meaning and relevance for social welfare organization. In addition, explaining the etiology of elder abuse contributes knowledge to larger policy issues which relate to the family providing care for elderly members.

EARLY RESEARCH

There have been several investigations of elder abuse since 1978. Many are not well-recognized, because they have not been published, use very small samples or lack sophisticated techniques for data collection and analysis. These include surveys of service providers (McLaughlin et al, 1980; Reynolds and Stanton, 1983; Jacobs and Dentel, 1984) along with case analyses of hospitalized abuse victims or those receiving community-based services (Steur and Austin, 1980; Anastasio, 1981; O'Malley et al, 1984; Environmental factors precipitate abuse, 1984). In addition, many state and local departments of human services or aging, especially those in states with adult protective service or elder abuse reporting laws, have maintained records on reported instances of elder abuse and presented them in summary form at conferences and Congressional hearings (e.g., U.S. Select Committee on Aging, 1981, 1985).

There are ten well-recognized attempts to systematically research elder abuse. Those published prior to 1982 primarily try to demonstrate the existence of elder abuse as a problem as well as describe its nature and scope.

Using various methodologies, from case analysis (Rathbone-McCuan, 1978; Lau and Kosberg, 1979) to surveys of service providers and sometimes elderly persons themselves (O'Malley et al, 1979; Douglass et al, 1979; Block and Sinnott, 1979; Chen et al, 1981), this early research suggests that at least four percent of the general elderly population are abused, neglected or exploited annually, with increased incidence to ten percent of those elderly persons who are frail and impaired. The studies also present a profile of the abused elder as typically female, very old, physically or mentally impaired and either living alone or with the abuser, on whom she is dependent.

The early researchers on elder abuse rarely investigated the etiology of the problem. Rather, they speculated on the subject through analogy with child abuse and spouse abuse. As a result, they offer laundry lists of possible explanations.

Overviews on the elder abuse published in 1982 or before reflect the speculations of those early researchers. They imply that the causes of elder abuse are multiple, diverse and unrelated. Villmoare and Bergman (1981), for example, in their guide for practitioners and policy makers, summarize the leading theories on the causes of elder abuse to date as follows: (1) impairment of the elder, which increases dependency on and vulnerability to others and may lead to learned helplessness; (2) individual pathologies of the abuser, including mental illness, retardation and alcoholism; (3) internal family dynamics, such as learned patterns of violence and the stress of caregiving; (4) external stress, illustrated by income and employment status; (5) demographic and social changes which result in increased numbers of frail elders placing excessive demands on families; and (6) stereotypic and prejudiced attitudes toward elderly and disabled persons that serve to justify their maltreatment. The overview of the U.S. House Select Committee on Aging (1981) summary publication on elder abuse hearings offers a dozen dominant causes: ageism, retaliation, violence as a way of life, lack of close family ties, lack of financial resources, lack of community resources, resentment of dependency, increased life expectancy, history of personal and mental problems, unemployment, history of alcohol and drug abuse problems, environmental conditions and an emphasis on caregiver stress overall. Finally, Pedrick-Cornell and Gelles (1982), in critiquing current research and reports on the subject, offer three major factors associated with abuse occurrence: (1) physical or mental impairment on the part of the elder, (2) stress of caregiving for the abuser, and (3) intergenerational use of violence to resolve conflict.

The early research on elder abuse was characterized by methodological and other problems. Uniformly these included vague and overly broad operational definitions, nonrandom samples and a failure to distinguish between the various forms of abuse in conclusions. Occasionally, the studies were also limited by low survey response rates (O'Malley et al, 1979; Block and Sinnott, 1979; Chen et al, 1981) and tying generalized respondent perceptions to specific variables (Douglass et al, 1979; Block and Sinnott, 1979).

RECENT RESEARCH

The four studies of elder abuse published in 1982 or later do not limit their primary focus to the nature and scope of the problem. Instead, they attempt to test hypotheses and assumptions on the causes of elder abuse generated in the early studies.

Sengstock and Liang (1982) use a variety of techniques including questionnaires and interviews of service providers, to identify and collect information on 77 cases of elder abuse in the Detroit metropolitan area. Interviews are also conducted with 20 abuse victims, with special emphasis given to stress as causing the abuse (Sengstock et al, 1982).

Steinmetz and Amsden (1983) employ a snowball technique to obtain a sample of filial caregivers to elderly persons. They then conduct semi-structured interviews with the caregivers with a focus on stress and dependency as precipitators to abuse.

Phillips (1983) interviews a purposive sample of 74 elderly persons identified from the active caseloads of public health nurses in Arizona as having either a "good relationship" or an abusive relationship with their caregivers. She is specifically interested in the differences or similarities between the two groups with respect to such factors as social networks, caregiver stress and caregiver-elder age discrepancies.

Wolf et al (1984) collect information on elder abuse from three federally-funded model projects in Massachusetts, New York and Rhode Island. Data collection includes assessment of 328 abuse cases and 49 comparison nonabuse cases, two surveys of 212 community agencies, case studies of the model projects, and in-depth interviews with 42 physically abused elders and 42 matched control cases. The last aspect of their research is particularly interesting for its inquiry into the etiology of elder abuse. Many of the interview questions specifically relate to possible explanations of elder abuse of interest to this study, i.e., mental illness or impairment of the abuser, exposure of the abuser to family violence during childhood, caregiver stress, dependency of the abuser on the elderly victim, external stress on the family and social isolation of the family.

The recent studies of elder abuse represent improvements over their predecessors in terms of problem conceptualization and research design. This particularly applies to those undertaken by Philips and Wolf et al, who for the first time use comparison groups in exploring abuse etiology.

Nonetheless, there are still a number of limitations characterizing the recent research, First, no study to date has interviewed the perpetrators in order to identify abuse etiology. Therefore, at best, research has depended on second (victim) or third (caseworker) hand perceptions of etiology. Second, little research to date has attempted to collect information using either a restricted definition of abuse (exception: Wolf et al) or restricted abuser group (exception: Steinmetz and Amsden) and none has done so with respect to both. There is, however, reason to believe that the various forms of abuse and different categories of perpetrators are associated with different abuse etiologies (O'Malley et al, 1984). Third, no research to date has sequentially refined its understanding of abuse etiology through repeated inquiry using the same respondents. As a result, the meaning of salient abuse factors has remained superficially understood at best.

EXISTING THEORY

The literature suggests five dominant explanations for elder abuse. Four relate to the perpetrator (i.e., abuse socialization, pathology, stress and social isolation) and one to the victim (i.e., vulnerability).

Abuse Socialization

The first explanation suggests that some persons have been socialized to abuse elders through learning proabuse norms and antielder attitudes during childhood. This explanation is based on social learning theory.

Support for learning abuse by observing or participating in the activity comes from a series of experiments wherein children and young adults imitate the behavior of aggressive models (Liebert and Baron,

1972; Bandura, 1973). In addition, it is found in the child abuse literature, wherein a "cycle of abuse" is frequently noted (for a review on the
subject see Gelles and Straus, 1979). A "cycle of abuse" was also a finding of Straus et al's (1980) national survey on family violence, and
Walker's (1983) and Fagan et al's (1983) studies of battered women.

In the elder abuse literature, there is widespread belief that children
who are abused grow up to abuse their parents in old age (e.g., Briley,
1979; U.S. Senate Special Committee on Aging, 1980). More direct
support comes from the following research on elder abuse:
(1) Rathbone-McCuan (1978) found the majority of the cases she analyzed had a history of inter- or intra-generational conflict. (2) Lau and
Kosberg (1979) noted instances of violence across generations in the
cases they studied. (3) Douglass et al (1979) found more practitioners
agreeing with the statement, "A child who is abused or witnesses abuse
grows up to be an abusive adult," than with any of the other three hy-
pothesized causal explanations. (4) Chen et al (1981) discovered 60.0
percent of the practitioners they surveyed held the belief that abusive
families have lifestyles wherein there is a general acceptance of violence.
(5) Sengstock and Liang (1982) found that nearly half of their respondents considered force appropriate in families to settle disputes.

On the other hand, Wolf et al (1984) did not find an association between child abuse and elder abuse. The abused elders in their sample
did not report more physical punishment as children than did the nonabused elders. Moreover, they did not indicate that the perpetrator had
been abused as a child.

Support for the existence of ageism is ample (Butler, 1975; Harris
and Associates, 1975; Thomas, 1981; Achenbaum, 1983). One poll indicated that the public's image of old people is that of "senile, lonely,
used-up bodies, rotting away and waiting to die" (Troll and Nowak,
1976, p. 42). There is also evidence that the effect of ageism is the dehumanization of elders (Butler and Lewis, 1973). There, however, has
been no research specifically on the association of elder abuse and ageism. Ageism, nonetheless, has been widely suggested as providing a
cultural backdrop conducive for abuse occurrence (Block and Sinnott,
1979; U.S. House Select Committee on Aging, 1981).

Pathology

According to this explanation, elder abuse occurs because of pathology or aberrant mental functioning on the part of the perpetrator. Aber-

rant mental functioning can happen as a result of developmental disability, mental retardation, mental illness, substance abuse or defective personality. Once present, it can decrease an individual's tolerance for frustration and ability to control aggressive behavior. Alternatively, it can increase an individual's tolerance for abuse infliction by giving abuse special meaning and value for itself.

Pathology has been a major explanation for child abuse and spouse abuse (Kempe et al, 1962; Steele and Pollock, 1974; Blumberg, 1974; Faulk, 1974; Shainess, 1975; Walker, 1979; Sanchez-Dirks, 1979). Others in the field, however, severely criticize this approach for its failure to generate supportive empirical research and its failure to identify the specific abnormalities associated with abuse (Gelles, 1974). It is true that a number of studies exist which suggest that mentally ill and mentally retarded people are not more violent than others (for a review see Monahan, 1981). What is less clear from these studies is the role of pathology in association with factors which generate stress and frustration in triggering abuse occurrence.

A number of sources mention pathology as a possible cause of elder abuse (e.g., Langley, 1981; Rathbone-McCuan and Hashimi, 1982; Giordano and Giordano, 1984). Support for it as an explanation for elder abuse has gradually emerged through empirical investigation. Rathbone-McCuan (1978) found a history of alcoholism, retardation or psychotic illness for either the caregiver or elder in the majority of abuse case histories she analyzed. Lau and Kosberg (1979, p. 13) uncovered instances of "non-normal" caregivers.

> These are situations where parents have cared for schizophrenic, retarded, or alcoholic children. As aged parents weaken and need care, these adult children become abusing and neglectful caregivers because of an inability to make appropriate judgments and perceptions.

The service providers surveyed by Douglass et al (1979) identified substance abuse as the second leading cause of elder abuse in response to an open-ended question on its origins. Those in Chen et al's (1981) study also mentioned an immature personality, personality or character disorder, substance abuse or unresolved family conflict as dominant factors to becoming an abuser.

Among recent research studies, there is divergence of findings with respect to the association between pathology and elder abuse. Sengstock and Liang (1982) found that pathology did not play a role in the majority of cases they analyzed, although it was evident in a few and these cases tended to represent relatively serious problems. In contrast, Wolf et al (1984) report individual pathology as a major correlate of elder abuse. In comparing abused elders with nonabused elders they found abused elders were three times more likely to indicate that their abusers had mental or emotional problems than were the nonabused elders. Interviews with their caseworkers also revealed the abusing caregivers more likely to have a history of psychotic hospitalization (37.5% versus 0.5%), more likely to be alcoholic (56.3% versus 9.4%), and more likely to be drug users (5.7% versus 0.0%).

Stress

Another explanation of elder abuse surrounds stress experienced by the abusing caregiver. According to this explanation, abuse occurs because of stress overload. The source of this stress may be internal or external to the caregiving relationship. When it is internal, it relates to the strain or sometimes burden of caring for a dependent elderly family member. When the source of stress is external to the caregiving relationship, it relates to environmental circumstances or family life crisis events. In either case, stress overload occurs when an individual's skills or resources are found wanting with respect to perceived or actual response to impinging demands (Mechanic, 1983). Stress overload means that the demands have exceeded the adaptive resources of the caregiver or the caregiver's family system.

Family stress theory has its origins in Hill's (1949, 1958) classic research on war-induced separation and reunion. Hill attempted to show the amount of change induced in the family system based on the hardships inherent in stressor events. Some researchers have suggested that any change in life pattern can be stressful (Holmes and Rahe, 1967; Dohrenwend, 1974). However, many more have held that only negative or undesirable changes are stressful (Gersten et al, 1974; Vinokur and Selzer, 1975; Johnson and Sarason, 1979).

There seem to be a number of factors which determine the impact of the stressor event on the individual or system. Besides the undesirability of the event, these include individual vulnerability (Appley and Trumbull, 1967); social structures that prepare, motivate and support adaptive responses (Mechanic, 1970); psychological and other moderators (Johnson and Sarason, 1979); volume of change (Makosky, 1982); and perception of hardship (Lundberg et al, 1975; Hurst et al, 1978).

Finally, it is suggested that stress can have an accumulative effect over time (Holmes and Masuda, 1974; Paykel and Tanner, 1976). This has led some theorists to distinguish between acute stress and chronic stress. In this distinction, acute stress is shorter term and reduced once the threat or danger has passed. Chronic stress is longer term, and various problems result from the individual's resources being taxed for so long a period (Farmer et al, 1984).

A potential source of stress is internal to the caregiving relationship. The nature of the tasks performed and the intimacy required for much caregiving can cause both acute and chronic strain for caregivers.

Families remain connected to elderly members. They do not abandon them as the financial, psychological, social or physical needs of the elders increase (Shanas, 1979; Branch and Jette, 1983; Soldo and Myllyluoma, 1983; Sangl, 1985). Indeed, families are the primary caregivers to dependent elders living in the community. The General Accounting Office's study of elderly Cleveland residents reveals that family and friends provide 50.0 percent of the services to older persons at all levels of functioning, and nearly 80.0 percent for those who are severely impaired (Comptroller General of the United States, 1977). Brody (1977) estimates that 70.0 to 80.0 percent of this care is provided specifically by adult offspring. In fact, the ability of dependent elders to remain in the community is often dependent on the caregiving efforts of family members, especially adult children (Cantor, 1975; Palmore, 1976; Brody et al, 1978).

There is considerable agreement that the role of caregiver to an impaired elder can be stressful or burdensome (Simos, 1973; Eggert et al, 1977; Miller, 1981; Cantor, 1983; Reece et al, 1983; Baines, 1984; Ory, 1985). Most existing research, however, suggests that whether or not caregiving is actually stressful or burdensome relates to a number of specific factors, such as: (1) frequency and distress of elder behaviors (Davies et al, 1985); (2) competing tasks demands (Rankin and Pinkston, 1985); (3) type of caregiving task performed (Fumich and Poulshock, 1981); (4) functional status of the elder (Perrotta, 1984); (5) dangerous or odd behavior or lack of cooperation by the elder (Lowenthal, 1964; Sainsbury and Grad de Alarcon, 1970); (6) insufficient time or money (Baumhover and Meherg, 1982); or (7) some combination of specific factors (Poulshock and Deimling, 1984). Springer and Brubaker (1984) provide a list of situations which produce stress for the caregiver of an elderly person. The list includes lack of necessary services and supplies for the elder, lack of space with a resident elder, time and decision management requirements and role shifts for adult offspring and dependent elder. Researchers agree that although most caregivers are stressed sometimes, only a few are often severely stressed (Benjamin Rose Institute, 1982; Cicirelli, 1981, 1983).

External stress is viewed by many as a major contributor to child abuse and spouse abuse (Gil, 1971; Gelles, 1974; Straus, 1980a; Straus et al, 1980). Those who hold this view cite such stressor events as poverty, unemployment, accidents and illnesses as causing abuse.

Likewise, stress internal to the caregiving relationship is considered a factor in explaining child abuse (Herrenkohl and Herrenkohl, 1981). Garbarino and Gilliam (1980), for example, discuss the role of the child in abuse, citing a variety of studies which suggest caregiving can be particularly stressful and abuse may result if the child is seen as "different" or "difficult" or if the child is unwanted.

In the elder abuse literature, stress is an extremely popular explanation for elder abuse (e.g., Brown, 1979-1980; U.S. House Select Committee on Aging, 1981). Research to support this comes from a variety of sources.

Support for external stress as an explanation for elder abuse comes from the following: (1) Chen et al (1981), who found family stress or crisis the most frequently mentioned cause of elder abuse among all practitioners surveyed; and (2) Sengstock et al (1982), who reported that 85.0 percent of the abused elders they surveyed had experienced five or more stressful events during the previus year, 50.0 percent had experienced ten or more, and 20.0 percent 19 or more stressful events. Wolf et al (1984), in contrast, did not find any significant differences between the abusing and nonabusing caregivers for their sample of elderly subjects with respect to the following life crisis events: death of someone close, divorce, marriage, arrest, separation, unemployment, retirement, residence change and household addition.

Support for stress internal to the caregiving relationship being associated with elder abuse also comes from a number of studies, including: (1) O'Malley et al (1979), who found that the service providers they surveyed considered the elder as a source of stress to the abuser in 63.0 percent of the 183 abuse citings; (2) Douglass et al (1979), who found the caregiver's inability to deal with the elder's dependency needs as a frequently cited cause of elder abuse by service providers surveyed; and (3) Steinmetz and Amsden (1983), who discovered in their sample of caregivers a significant relationship between threats of physical force and demanding elders, as well as physical abuse and the elder's level of mental health dependency. In contrast, Phillips (1983) did not find a difference in stress between abused elders and those having a "good relationship" with their caregivers in her sample of elderly subjects.

Social Isolation

Social support is frequently identified as an important moderator to life stress and pathology (Kaplan et al, 1977; House, 1981; Cobb, 1982; D'Augelli, 1983). The caring and comfort of significant others has been found to effect stress reduction in a variety of situations (Jones, 1968; Caplan, 1974; Henderson, 1977; Wilcox, 1981). Family violence is one such situation. Numerous studies suggest that those without social support are more likely to abuse their children or their spouses when faced with life crises (Gelles, 1972; Justice and Justice, 1976; Maden and Wrench, 1977; Gottlieb, 1980; Garbarino and Gilliam, 1980). Similarly, symptoms of psychological impairment are stronger in situations in life crisis when individuals have low levels of social support (for a review of research on this subject see Cobb, 1976; Mueller, 1980; Greenblatt et al, 1982).

Social isolation, the absence of social support, is thought to contribute to elder abuse in several ways (Rathbone-McCuan and Hashimi, 1982). Isolation forces caregivers to cope with stress or crisis alone. It limits their ability to obtain assistance when needed. Moreover, isolation removes the presence of interested outsiders who can make the occurrence of abuse difficult, through potential intervention or contact with authorities.

More recent research on elder abuse suggests the importance of social isolation as a contributor to abuse occurrence. Chen et al (1981) found lack of adequate social and emotional support and community resources as causes of elder abuse in the estimation of 53.0 percent of practitioners surveyed. Sengstock and Liang (1982) discovered that the abused elders in their sample had few contacts with persons outside of their household. Although Phillips (1983) did not find any significant difference between the abused and nonabused elders in her sample in terms of number of individuals providing support and assistance, she did, however, note that the abused elders perceived less overall support from those involved in their social networks. Finally, Wolf et al (1984) found the abused elders in their sample had fewer overall contacts and were less satisfied with those they did have. Nonetheless, they were not less likely to have someone available to help if they required it. Based on these findings, Pillemer (1985) suggested that the critical variable for abuse occurrence may be the amount of involvement of outsiders in the home of the abuse victim. "The greater this involvement, the less easily a relative can be abusive without incurring the cost of negative sanctions from others" (p. 3).

Vulnerability

The last explanation of elder abuse to be discussed is vulnerability on the part of the elderly person. Vulnerability relates to the increased potential of some elders becoming abuse victims by virture of characteristics on their part which (1) increase their dependency on others and so the related stress of addressing that dependency, or (2) decrease their ability or willingness to guard against or escape from abuse occurrence. The origins of these characteristics may be within the physical, psychological, emotional, social or structural circumstances of the elder.

Vulnerability as an explanation for abuse occurrence is found in the literature on other maltreated populations, especially children. Gelles (1974) found younger children more likely to be abused than older children because of their lack of physical durability and the fact that parents cannot "reason" with them yet. Other studies have concurred that the usual period for child abuse is during the infancy and toddler stage (Solomon, 1973; Blumberg, 1974; Maden and Wrench, 1977; Gil, 1979; Straus et al, 1980). Helfer's (1973) causal model of child abuse includes as one of three essential components "a special kind of child," by virture of prematurity, mental retardation or birth defects. Other researchers also report that abused children frequently are premature or hypersensitive babies (Harrington, 1972; Hunter et al, 1978; Burgess, 1979) or have various kinds of deformities or developmental problems (Johnson and Morse, 1968; Zalba, 1971; for a review see Friedrich and Boriskin, 1976).

Support for this explanation is found in some of the elder abuse literature. In her case analysis Ratherbone-McCuan (1978) discovered that the majority of victims were dependent because of inadequate resources or functional limitations. Other early investigators found that at least three-fourths of their sample of abused elders were physically or mentally impaired (Lau and Kosberg, 1979; Block and Sinnott, 1979; O'Malley et al, 1979; Steur and Austin, 1980). Moreover, Douglass et al (1979) and Chen et al (1981) discovered functional dependency and vulnerability were important explanations for elder abuse among practitioner respondents.

More recent research on elder abuse does not emphasize vulnerability as an explanation. Although the abused elders in Sengstock and Liang's (1982) sample were mostly low income, they tended to be unimpaired. Phillips (1983) found no significant difference in physical functioning, or level of physical functioning and level of abuse, between abused and nonabused elders. Finally, Wolf et al's (1984) sample of abused elders did not differ from their sample of nonabused elders in terms of serious illness, recent hospitalization or recent decline in health status. In most respects, they did not differ in functional incapacity as well. Where there was a difference, however, abused elders were found to be less impaired than nonabused elders. They also saw themselves as less dependent and less in need of assistance than did nonabused elders.

Exchange Theory

Vulnerability to elder abuse can originate in the elder's inability or unwillingness to adequately reciprocate adult offspring for care provided. The resulting imbalance in exchange relations between elder and filial caregiver can promote or serve to justify abuse occurrence.

Exchange theory as a specific explanation for elder abuse has a checkered history. First suggested by Kosberg (1980), the theory was left unexamined until the recent writings of Wolf et al (1984).

Exchange theory basically holds that interaction between individuals is guided by the pursuit of rewards (benefits) and the avoidance of punishments (costs). The extension of benefits from one individual to another obligates the receiver to reciprocate in order for interaction to continue (Homans, 1961; Blau, 1968).

Applied to elder abuse, this explanation suggests that adult offspring (or others) provide care to dependent elders so long as the demands of care do not exceed the emotional gratification and other benefits (financial, for example) derived from care. When the costs of care outweigh the benefits and there are few alternatives outside of maintaining the situation as is (institutional placement of the elder, for instance, may be unacceptable or unaffordable), then the offspring may resort to elder abuse.

Exchange theory has been applied to the changing status of elderly persons (Dowd, 1975; Sussman, 1976) and the caregiving experience involving elderly persons and their families (Horowitz and Shindelman, 1981). It also has been applied to other forms of family violence. The classic explanation by Goode (1971) explores the deterrant value of force or its threat in maintaining the family power system. Edwards and Brauburger (1973) examine exchange between parents and their adolescent children in middle class families. Not only do they find that an exchange system exists, but also that the breakdown of exchange results in conflict and the use of overt control techniques. Finkelhor (1983), in identifying common features of family violence, notes that abuse may occur to compensate for a perceived lack or loss of power. Finally, Gelles (1983) suggests that abuse can happen in families when the principle of distributive justice is violated. According to this principle, people expect to be appropriately rewarded for their activities (Homans, 1961). When they are not, as can occur in situations of functional dependency, abuse may be the by-product.

LIMITATIONS OF VARIOUS ABUSE EXPLANATIONS

Each explanation of elder abuse has its limitations. The socialization approach does not account for behavioral differentials—abuse and otherwise—among individuals from the same or similar settings. In addition, it does not explain the particular timing of abuse occurrence. The pathological approach also does not explain the timing of abuse. Furthermore, it does not identify the conditions which result in a manifestation of pathology as abuse rather than some other type of behavior or emotion. The stress approach is limited in not differentiating among caregivers—nearly all of whom are stressed—those who abuse and those who do not. Social isolation at best makes sense only in conjunction with some other explanation of abuse occurrence. Finally, vulnerability as an explanation is limited by its inability to account for the adoption of abuse over some other response in situations characterized by dependency or lack of reciprocity and lack of alternatives.

It is clear not only from this analysis but also from the inconsistencies among research findings for any particular explanation that only a conceptual framework which integrates salient factors offers any meaningful explanation for elder abuse. No single factor tells the whole story. No listing of factors lends understanding to this complex phenomenon.

CONCEPTUAL FRAMEWORKS FOR EXPLAINING ELDER ABUSE

There is widespread recognition that family abuse is a multifaceted problem demanding multifaceted explanation (e.g., Gil, 1970; Block and Sinnott, 1979). However, there have been few attempts at such explanation. Only a handful of attempts emerge from the literature on child abuse and spouse abuse (Straus, 1973; Justice and Justice, 1976;

Garbarino, 1976, 1977). In the literature on elder abuse three conceptual frameworks have been suggested for integrating the various factors found associated with abuse occurrence.

The first, offered by Kosberg (1979, 1980), focuses on a human ecology model of elder abuse. This model was originally applied to explaining child abuse by Garbarino (1976, 1977). It indicates that for abuse to occur there must be cultural acceptance of the use of force as well as social perception of the victims as "less worthy." In addition, the caregiver must be isolated from potential support. Under these conditions, abuse results from role incompetence on the part of the caregiver. Role incompetence results from lack of experience in rehearsing the role of caregiver, a lack of knowledge and the presence of unrealistic expectations regarding the caregiver role, or a failure on the part of the caregiver to reorder personal priorities.

In the second model, Hickey (1979) emphasizes developmental dysfunctions which render some persons incapable of sustaining personal relations in the context of family. Given this backdrop, abuse occurs in the presence of situational or environmental conditions, such as inadequate income, which increase tension in the domestic setting.

The third and most recent conceptual framework for explaining elder abuse is offered by Phillips (1983). She is the only one to have tested her model through empirical research. Phillips' model has three stages. The first, "defining the situation," represents the means by which the background of interchange between elder and caregiver was determined. This includes self-assessed social networks, self-assessed activities of daily living and family structure. Stage two, "cognitive process," represents the unconscious process of elder and caregiver that results in the assignment of role identities. This includes the role that one devises for self as well as expectations and perceptions of the other person. Stage three, "expressive process," represents the way the elder and caregiver express their roles in either behavior or mood states. Possible expressions include abuse, anxiety, depression or anger. In testing her model Phillips found that the elder's perception of the caregiver contributed negatively, and family members in the household and available to help contributed positively to explaining 54.0 percent of the variance in the abuse variable. Elder perception of caregiver was a composite based on the age of the elder and the number of friends who call on the phone. The lower the elder's age and higher the number of friends who call on the phone, the higher the elder's perception of the caregiver's behavior.

Each of the existing conceptual frameworks for explaining elder abuse is deficient in certain important respects. Kosberg's human ecology framework fails to account for the timing of abuse occurrence as well as the possible influence of pathological characteristics on the part of the caregiver in contributing to elder abuse. Hickey's emphasis on developmental dysfunction coupled with environmental conditions does not explain the influence of cultural variables in abuse occurrence. Cultural variables, for example, account for the different incidence of elder abuse among Americans whose socialization include the learning of proabuse norms and antielder attitudes and the Semais of Malaya whose socialization includes the learning of antiabuse norms and proelder attitudes (Dentan, 1968; Gil, 1974). Finally, Phillips' conceptual framework is only a skeleton explanation for elder abuse. It lacks substance and essential linkages. Accordingly, it leaves unanswered many questions, including: What triggers abuse? Why does abuse also occur in homes where there are family members available to help and the elder is fairly young and in contact with friends? (Sengstock and Liang, 1982).

CHAPTER II

THE CONCEPTUAL FRAMEWORK

OVERVIEW

IN REVIEWING the literature it became evident that several constructs held promise for further exploration on the etiology of elder abuse. Briefly, these constructs are: abuse socialization, stress, social isolation and pathology for the abuser; and vulnerability for the elder. Although no construct was uniformly supported by existing research, each received broad enough support for considered explanation of the phenomenon. The absence of uniform support may reflect the usual presentation of these constructs as independent and unrelated. It is more likely that they are interdependent. Our understanding of other forms of family violence as well as complex matters in general suggests that elder abuse originates from neither a single cause nor a set of unrelated causes.

The intent of this study is to explore to what extent these factors contribute to elder abuse by filial caregivers. In order to meaningfully study them, however, a conceptual framework is proposed which offers a set of relations between the factors that can be tested through research.

The conceptual framework of this study represents a unique combination of existing theoretical approaches, with primary emphasis on social learning and secondary emphasis on stress and pathology. In general, it suggests that a behavioral response requires knowledge about the response, acquired through the process of learning, as well as incentive for imitation of the response. Incentive for imitation of the response requires conditions internal or external to the individual which dispose the individual in the direction of imitating that response as well as a specific event to activate these conditions in such a manner that the individual actually does initiate the response.

The conceptual framework is based on a number of assumptions. First, the individual is social. By virtue of a social nature, the individual interacts with groups and it is through group interaction that socialization occurs. Second, the individual begins life without behavioral responses. Rather, the individual learns behavioral responses as a result of a socialization process which includes certain responses as normative activities. Third, learned behavioral responses have the potential of being generalized beyond the original learning context. The generalization process results from the individual's ability to perceive situations as sufficiently similar to warrant similar responses. Fourth, behavioral responses require stimuli for their occurrence. Moreover, a previously evoked behavioral response may serve as conditioning for future similar response occurrences. Fifth, an emotional response can remain internal or be externalized in the form of a behavioral response. An emotional response will trigger a behavioral response when the individual's ability to keep internal the response has diminished.

This conceptual framework has application for understanding elder abuse as a behavioral response on the part of the filial caregiver. Accordingly, learning abuse is likely to result from exposure to related socially sanctioned acts during childhood which are seen as rewarding. Learning to regard elders as recipients for abuse infliction is likely to result from exposure to their portrayal as qualitatively different than most persons by virtue of possessing characteristics that are not culturally valued. Having been socialized to regard abuse as a possible expression of frustration, and elders as less than human, elder abuse is likely under the following conditions alone or in combination: First, chronic structural or contextual factors affecting the caregivers increase the level of stress experienced by the caregivers. Second, the caregivers may possess pathological characteristics which increase their tolerance for abuse affliction or decrease their tolerance for stress. Third, structural or contextual factors or characteristics on the part of the elder increase the elder's vulnerability to abuse or decrease the elder's likelihood of retaliating against abuse. In addition, the caregivers must perceive themselves under conditions of acute stress resulting from events that may or may not directly relate to the situation of providing care to the elder in order for abuse to occur.

Chronic structural or contextual factors which may increase the level of stress experienced by caregivers include insufficient respite, inadequate social support, insufficient income, health problems, crowded living conditions, caregiver role incompetence, role satiation, greed for valuables held by the elder, and perception of the elder as interfering with the independence needs of the caregivers. Pathological characteristics which may increase the tolerance of caregivers for abuse infliction or decrease their tolerance for stress include physical or mental abnormality or impairment, alcohol or other drug abuse, unacceptance of role reversal, unresolved family conflict, and having a self-concept as "abusive." Structural or contextual factors or characteristics of elders which may increase their vulnerability to abuse or decrease their likelihood of retaliating against abuse include economic dependence, a devalued self-concept with old age, physical or mental impairment, the absence or ineffectiveness of or ignorance about laws or services protective in nature, the elder's unwillingness to disrupt relations with the caregivers, and the elder's desire to save face.

EXPLAINING THE CONCEPTUAL FRAMEWORK

Explaining the conceptual framework of this study begins with the learning of abuse as a behavioral response. Tendencies toward abuse develop as a result of socialization which includes abuse as normative activity. The acceptability of this activity for later imitation depends on the legitimacy of the activity source and the perceived reward for activity imitation. Important activity sources or agents of socialization during childhood include parents and other persons regarded as authority figures and with whom there is regular contact. These provide the foci for much of childhood learning around cultural norms. To the extent that these agents emphasize abuse infliction, children are likely to regard the activity as socially sanctioned (otherwise, why would these important references emphasize the activity) and appropriate under certain circumstances. Imitation is likely to follow if the individual also considers abuse infliction to facilitate the achievement of personally desired goals, such as docility on the part of the victim when the victim is seen as irritating.

This same process applies to the learning of antielder attitudes. In other words, antielder attitudes result from conformity to a social milieu that is prejudiced toward persons by virtue of their age and that overgeneralizes the attributes of these persons. The origins of these attitudes may rest in economic and social competition or other such phenomena but their usual acquisition on the individual level is through association with significant others who hold them. Acceptance of these attitudes by the individual is likely to follow under two conditions. First, the individual has no source of information which is regarded as more acceptable and legitimate and which provides information of a variant nature. Second, the individual is rewarded, perhaps through social acceptance, for having the attitudes.

Explaining the conceptual framework also requires examining the situation of providing care to an elderly relative, a situation which can strain the caregiving capacities of family members. Often the elder is disabled and requires assistance in activities of daily living, which can be a source of mental and physical exertion for the caregiver. The strain can increase when the caregiver has little respite from or social support for these activities. Moreover, the caregiver may likewise be ill or impaired and unable to care for someone else except at considerable personal cost. Other times the caregiver may be incapable of providing the kind of care required by an infirm elder. Tasks such as changing catheters or arranging special diets may be difficult for individual caregivers, and failure to adequately accomplish them may prove frustrating. Often times the cost of caring for an elderly relative can strain an already limited household budget.

Crowded living conditions made more crowded by the addition of an elderly relative to the household also can generate tensions throughout the family. Sometimes the caregiver is simply overwhelmed by virtue of the many and varied demands that arise from being a caregiver as well as being perhaps homemaker, worker, spouse and parent. Finally, the caregiver may experience strain as a result of conflict with the elder. In this regard, the elder may not part with pension or other benefits despite the receipt of care from the family member. Especially when these funds are needed to maintain the household, failure to relinquish them may seriously frustrate the caregiver. Moreover, in situations where the caregiver has finally achieved a measure of independence, such as when teenage children leave home for college, the addition of a frail and impaired elder may be frustrating, since it conflicts with the perceived independence needs of the caregiver.

Some caregivers have lowered tolerance for stress as a result of abnormality, impairment, substance abuse or personality characteristics. In the last regard, uneasiness can arise over role reversals, as children assume responsibility for their parents. Unresolved family conflicts can cause emotions to smolder and then flare. Finally, the caregiver may take pride in being the kind of person who manages "to keep things in order," in which case perceived "lack of order" may cause more vehement reaction than for someone without this self-concept. Perceived lack of order can result from feces smeared on the walls by a confused and incontinent elder at one extreme, or from medicine bottles lining the counter for an ill elder at the other extreme.

Similar characteristics as these can increase a caregiver's tolerance for abuse infliction. For example, the caregiver who has pride in "keeping things in order" may sometimes find abuse simply an expedient means for reaching the greater goal of "maintained order." A caregiver intoxicated by alcohol may feel less inhibited with inflicting abuse. Another who is mentally retarded may not understand the probable effect of abuse infliction on the victim. Finally, unresolved family conflict may serve to justify abuse infliction as a means for "righting wrongs once done."

Explaining the conceptual framework further requires examining the elder's vulnerability to abuse or inability or unwillingness to retaliate against repeated abuse occurrence. Seemingly the elder has a number of means available for protecting or retaliating against abuse occurrences. These include leaving the situation, seeking protection under the law and self-defense. The likelihood of the elder using any of these means depends on the elder's ability and desire to do so, which tend to decrease under certain circumstances. For example, the elder may not leave the situation because of a lack of economic resources to live anywhere else. Or the elder may be too frail and impaired to resist. The elder may have developed a devalued self-concept with old age; accordingly, the elder may believe that a "helpless, hopeless, old dependent" should be satisfied with any provisions made by family members. The elder may be unwilling to report the abuse to the police or other authorities either because of a desire to "save face" or out of family loyalty and affection for the caregiver. Finally, the elderly may be ignorant of domestic violence or adult protective laws and services that could help deal with the situation, or these laws and services may not exist or may only inadequately exist in the community.

Lastly, explaining the conceptual framework requires considering the acute stress experienced by the caregiver which actually serves to precipitate elder abuse. When caregivers have already been socialized toward elder abuse, when they themselves or the circumstances in which they find themselves are primed for abuse occurrence by virtue of rendering the caregivers less able to tolerate additional stress or more able to inflict abuse, and/or when the potential victim is vulnerable to abuse, then the stage has been set which allows what may be even a minimal amount of strain under other circumstances to be perceived as a major strain and to result in elder abuse.

In some cases, the source of the additional stress may be the elder. Perhaps the elder refuses to take prescribed medication. The caregiver initially tries to coax the elder into taking the medication, but when this fails and frustration occurs, abuse results. Perhaps the elder pushes the evening meal on the floor saying, "It doesn't taste right." The caregiver may have fixed the meal in a strained and exhausted state after a full day of work. Throwing the meal on the floor becomes "the last straw" and abuse occurs. In other cases, the sources of the additional stress may be something not directly related to the elder. Perhaps the caregiver is fired from employment and "takes out" this frustration on the elder in the form of abuse occurrence; in this regard the elder may be perceived as an additional household expense at a time when resources to cover these expenses are gone. Perhaps the caregiver falls while carrying the elder's needed oxygen into the house. Frustrated at being unable to complete the task in an easy and competent manner, the caregiver "scapegoats" the elder with abusive acts. In any case, the timing of this stress immediately or nearly immediately precedes abuse occurrence.

COMPARISON WITH OTHER EXPLANATIONS

The conceptual framework presented in this study is much advanced over approaches suggested in the literature that emphasize a single cause or set of unrelated causes. First, it underscores the fact that elder abuse is a process rather than a single act. The events culminating in abuse occurrence may begin in the childhood of the abuser, and they may involve forces as seemingly diverse as the burden of caregiving and financial need. Nonetheless, they represent a series of events or forces. The abuser does not commit the act of violence against an older person in a vacuum. Second, the conceptual framework identifies stages leading to abuse infliction. Stage one (abuse socialization), establishes the social sanctions; stage two (chronic stress, pathology or vulnerability), the characteristics peculiar to the abuser or elder; and stage three (acute stress), the particular event to trigger abuse occurrence. Stages indicate response as a result of the logical sequencing of events or forces. They imply that abuse does not "just happen." It has precondition or impetus.

The conceptual framework of this study also is much advanced over existing models for explaining elder abuse. First, it is the only one that considers both cultural and individual influences. Any explanation of elder abuse must include both in order to explain the occurrence of the phenomenon among some groups but not other groups, and among some individuals in the same group but not other individuals. Second, it alone identifies more than a single path leading to abuse occurrence. Our current understanding of abusers would suggest that they are not of one type, and the circumstances leading to abuse are not always the same. Third, the conceptual framework presented in this study is the only one that attempts to incorporate the factors explaining elder abuse found to be meaningful in the research on the subject to date. The others, by and large, have their origins in creative thought or in research on other abused populations.

RESEARCH QUESTIONS

Once again, the literature described in the last chapter indicated that certain factors are important in the etiology of elder abuse. For the abuser, these factors include: (1) socialization to elder abuse through ageism and learning proabuse norms, (2) stress overload as a result of factors internal or external to the caregiving relationship, and (3) pathology. For the elder, the factors include characteristics which render the elder vulnerable to abuse or unable to retaliate against it.

The conceptual framework of this study incorporates these factors and shows their possible interrelationships and linkage to abuse occurrence. Social isolation is the only factor described earlier which is not specifically addressed in the conceptual framework. Social isolation of the abuser is integral to the conceptual framework and was included in its description. However, as a moderator to stress or pathology, its relationship in the etiology of elder abuse is indirect rather than direct, thereby excluding its identification as a major factor for abuse occurrence.

It is the purpose of this study to explore the function of the above factors in explaining the physical abuse of elderly persons by their adult offspring. More specifically, the study attempts to answer the following questions: (1) What variables explain elder abuse by filial caregivers? (2) Do configurations emerge among the variables? (3) What meanings do caregivers attach to the variables?

If the conceptual framework presented in this study does explain elder abuse, then related research should demonstrate the following:

(1) In addition to being socialized to the acceptance of violence in the American context, the abuser may have grown up in an abusive family or subculture. (2) One or more of three situations occurred: (a) The abuser experienced considerable stress as a result of life crisis events, environmental conditions or elder care. (b) The abuser was pathological. (c) The elder had characteristics which rendered him or her vulnerable to abuse infliction. (3) A specific incident perceived as stressful to the abuser triggered the occurrence of abuse.

This study focuses on determining the adequacy of the conceptual framework in explaining elder abuse. Determining the adequacy of the conceptual framework requires exploring the various dimensions of each construct as they are revealed among adult offspring known to have abused their elderly parents. The next chapter describes the methodology employed to do this.

The construct of ageism, identified in the conceptual framework, is not examined in the study. Ageism may be important in explaining elder abuse. However, its importance lies in the cultural climate it creates which fosters the dehumanization and maltreatment of older persons. Since our's is an ageist society, and since all those who are members of this society are exposed to this attitude in varying degrees, for the purpose of the study, ageism is regarded as characteristic of all persons comprising the research sample.

DEFINITION OF TERMS

In this study "adult offspring" is defined as the son or daughter aged 18 years or more of an elder parent. The offspring relationship may originate through birth, adoption, foster care arrangement or marriage. An "elder" is a person aged 60 years or over. "Filial caregiver" is an adult offspring who assumes responsibility for the care of an elder parent as a result of family relationship. "Care" means services provided to an elder to meet the needs of daily living. "Abuse" (or "physical abuse") is the infliction of injuries or pain. As used in the conceptual framework for explaining elder abuse, "abuse socialization" is the process by which an individual learns norms or patterns which permit the use of abuse as a behavioral response within certain contexts. "Chronic stress" is defined as long term physical or mental strain or exertion resulting from environmental circumstances or social events which require life adjustment. "Acute stress" contrasts with chronic stress in that it is short term and results from temporary threat or danger. "External stress" originates in environmental circumstances or life crisis events, "internal stress" in the caregiving relationship between the adult offspring and elder parent. "Pathology" refers to patterns or impairments of the mind or body which decrease the individual's ability to satisfactorily function in social interaction as judged by self or others. The origins of these patterns or impairments may be biological, cultural, social or chemical.

"Social isolation" is defined as the perceived or actual absence of social support from significant others. Social support can be emotional or instrumental in nature. Finally, "vulnerability" means the decreased capacity on the part of an elder to resist abuse as a result of physical, mental, emotional or social impairment.

ORGANIZATION OF VARIABLES

Within the conceptual framework, the dependent variable is physical abuse of an elder parent by adult offspring. Independent variables are contained in each of the constructs of abuse socialization, pathology and stress for the adult offspring along with vulnerability for the elder parent. Social isolation is a moderator for pathology and stress.

For abuse socialization, the independent variables include history of being abused as a child and history of the observation of domestic violence. For pathology, they include substance abuse, mental illness, mental retardation and emotional distress. For stress, the independent variables include stressful life events, caregiving tasks performed and perceived as burdensome, and presence of disturbing behaviors on the part of the elder parent. For social isolation, they include infrequency of contact with others, help received and activity participation as well as perception of lacking social support. For vulnerability, the independent variables include living arrangements and physical and emotional health of the elder parent. In every instance, the variables for each construct represent the dimensions to be explored in this study in an attempt to understand the etiology of elder abuse by adult offspring.

CHAPTER III

METHODOLOGY

OVERVIEW

THIS STUDY attempts to determine the etiology of elder abuse by adult offspring. More specifically, it tries to identify the salient factors in abuse occurrence, thereby generating hypotheses for testing suggested theories for explaining elder abuse. Accordingly, the study explores the extent to which abuse socialization, stress, pathology and social isolation for the adult offspring and vulnerability for the elder parent influence the infliction of abuse. A conceptual framework was developed from the theoretical interrelationships among these factors. Exploratory research is required to examine the interrelationships, given the infancy stage of elder abuse recognition and investigation, as well as the fact that there has been no research to date specifically on the abuse perpetrators.

SETTING

This exploratory study was conducted in the six-county region of Northeast Ohio. Representative counties were Cuyahoga, Summit, Lorain, Lake, Geauga and Ashtabula. These counties reflect a mix of urban-suburban-rural settings. Moreover, they contain 26.5% of Ohio's elderly population (Ohio Data User's Center, 1985).

Twenty-one health and human service agencies and hospitals agreed to participate in the study by examining their case records toward the identification of abusing adult offspring. The local department of human services was among the participating organizations in each county. Additionally, in Cuyahoga County the participating organizations included the Medical Geropsychiatric Program of Lutheran Medical Center, Social Services Department and Chronic Illness Center of Cleveland Metropolitan General Hospital, Emergency Services of St. Vincent Charity Hospital and Health Center, Clark Help Center of West Side Community Mental Health Center, Nursing Home Ombudsman Program/Boarding Home Advocacy Program, Social Services Department of the Veteran's Administration, Lakewood Office of Aging, Westlake Office on Aging, Shaker Square Office of the Benjamin Rose Institute and various county and City of Cleveland criminal justice services, such as the Cuyahoga County Witness/Victim Service Center/ Domestic Violence Program and Cleveland Mediation Program.

The selection of the various participating organizations was based on three criteria. First, all county departments of human services in the region were included, since under Ohio's Protective Services Law for Adults they alone have mandated responsibility for receiving reports of elder abuse. Second, members of the Protective Services Consortium for Older Adults of Cuyahoga County were included if it was judged likely that they had contact with abusing adult offspring. The Consortium has 57 individual and organizational members. Its purpose is to prevent and treat elder abuse through community-wide networking, education, advocacy and planning. From 1984, when it began, through January, 1986 I served as director of the Consortium, and, therefore, was in a position to assess degree of contact with abuse perpetrators among Consortium members. Third, representatives of certain other service systems were approached to be participating organizations in the study, such as selected municipal offices on aging, in order to insure that major sectors serving elderly persons and their filial caregivers were represented.

All organizations contacted were willing to participate in the study, although only nine were ever able to identify qualifying adult offspring from their case records. These referral sources and the number of qualifying adult offspring they identified follow: Cuyahoga County Department of Human Services 18, Summit County Department of Human Services 6, Lorain County Department of Human Services 3, Geauga County Department of Human Services 1, Chronic Illness Center 5, Lutheran Medical Center 2, West Side Community Mental Health Center 2, Cuyahoga County Witness/Victim Service Center/Domestic Violence Program 1 and Nursing Home Ombudsman Program/ Boarding Home Advocacy Program 1. In addition, there was one self-referral, based on personal contact.

RESEARCH DESIGN AND SAMPLE

The design for this study was purposive comparison. Meaningful variables for explaining elder abuse by adult offspring were systematically identified and examined and their interrelationships explored through in-depth, focused interviews with a panel of abusing adult offspring. Essentially the approach was inductive, with an emphasis on discovering the etiology of elder abuse using existing theoretical perspectives set within a conceptual framework as the initial basis for inquiry, and later scrutinizing and reassessing the meaning of identified salient variables during a second interview with the panel of abusing adult offspring.

Purposive comparison was an appropriate research design given the state-of-the-art with respect to empirical research explaining elder abuse. As discussed earlier, many explanations for elder abuse are offered in the literature. However, they are usually provided as "laundry lists" of possible causes, without any effort made to prioritize or integrate them and without substantiation through empirical research. This design did not provide direct, time-ordered evidence of causality. It did, nonetheless, indicate independent variables that warranted further inquiry because of their demonstrated meaning within the context of elder abuse by adult offspring. This was useful, and appropriate for exploratory research. Given the relative lack of empirical research explaining elder abuse, especially the absence of research specifically on the abuse perpetrators, exploratory study was justified.

The research sample consisted of all adult offspring known to the study's referral sources who had physically abused an elder parent within the past 18 months. To be included in the sample, the abuse had to be verified according to one or more of the three criteria. The injuries or pain had to be (1) confirmed as physical abuse by the victim or perpetrator, (2) substantiated as physical abuse by third party observation, or (3) incompatible with the explanation or history provided by the victim or perpetrator.

Although this is not a random sample, there is no reason to suspect it is not representative of the situations of elder abuse that come to the attention of health and human service providers in states with elder abuse mandatory reporting laws. On the other hand, most abuse goes unreported and unacknowledged, never coming to the attention of authorities and service providers (U.S. House Select Committee on Aging, 1981). Furthermore, the choice of referring agencies and hospitals for this study was in part based on my having established positive working relations with their representatives while employed in public welfare and community planning as well as on my perception of their ability and willingness to cooperate in the research, factors which decrease their representativeness and increase the likelihood of bias.

The sampling method used in this study was justified. It provided suitable subjects for exploratory research on the etiology of elder abuse by adult offspring. It was accomplished with relative ease and little cost. Random sampling would not have been feasible. It would require too much time and research personnel. Moreover, there were no adequate resources for the identification of filial caregivers locally.

DATA COLLECTION

Data were collected in four stages. In the first stage, basic demographic and other information was obtained on all adult offspring identified by the referral sources that qualified for inclusion in the research by virtue of meeting the sample criteria. This information was acquired through interview with the caseworker of the elder parent or adult offspring at the referral source. With rare exception, caseworkers were social workers, counselors or public social services workers. In stages two and three, demographic data were obtained and variables for explaining elder abuse explored through interviews with qualifying adult offspring who were available, appropriate and willing to be interviewed. Finally, in stage four, the possible role of Appalachian culture in the etiology of some elder abuse was examined by interviewing selected representatives of that culture.

Consent to cooperate in the study had to be obtained at two levels. Initially the potential referral source had to agree to participate by identifying qualifying adult offspring. Consent was obtained at this level by meeting with agency or hospital administrators and explaining the purpose and procedures of the study as well as the particular safeguards made for subject confidentiality and anonymity of responses. This was facilitated by providing administrators with written description of the study, definition of key terms and sample letter of informed consent. The meeting with administrators was sometimes followed by conferences with clinical staff around the same matters. Adminstrators occasionally also had to receive clearance from agency or hospital attorneys or ethics committees before agreeing to participate.

Consent to cooperate from qualifying adult offspring was obtained first by the caseworker of the referral source and later by me, initially during telephone contact and subseqently during personal interview. After it was mutually agreed by the caseworker and myself that an adult offspring qualified for inclusion in the study and was available and appropriate for interview, the caseworker contacted the adult offspring to determine willingness to be interviewed. In so doing, the caseworker explained the nature of the research and the compensation to the adult offspring for participation. If the subject was willing to be interviewed, the caseworker gave me the individual's name, address and telephone number. I then proceeded to telephone the individual, describing the research in greater detail and obtaining a verbal consent to be interviewed. In addition, arrangements were made regarding the date, time and location for the interview. Finally, prior to answering any questions for the first interview, the subject signed a letter of informed consent, agreeing to the interview and acknowledging the various provisions of the research.

At every level, and by both representatives of the referral sources and myself, explanation of the study took the form of inviting adult offspring to answer questions during two interviews arranged at their convenience. The questions were said to surround what it is like to take care of and be around an elder parent, including the stresses and conflicts that can result. Adult offspring were cautioned that questions would only address past events and problems, and if they chose to reveal some current maltreatment of an elder, the interviewer would comply with the laws of the State of Ohio and report the situation to the local county department of human services.

In assessing whether or not a qualifying adult offspring should be asked to participate in the study, consideration was given to that individual's availability and appropriateness for interview. The adult offspring was not considered available if, according to the caseworker, the individual's whereabouts were unknown or she or he had moved out of Northeast Ohio, was institutionalized, would only communicate through an attorney, or would not permit any outside intervention or contact. The adult offspring was not considered appropriate for interview if, in the judgment of the caseworker and myself, the individual's pathology rendered her or him incapable of being interviewed, the individual or some other household member posed a danger to the elder parent or interviewer if the interview was conducted, or the interview would adversely affect present case planning by the referral source.

In order to maintain interest in the study and obtain as large a sample of qualifying adult offspring as was available through the participating agencies and hospitals, I kept in regular contact with representatives from each during the six-month data collection stage of the study, February through July, 1985. This was done by personal contacts, telephone calls or letters at intervals of no less than every two months (more often with organizations that proved to have larger numbers of identifiable qualifying adult offspring).

Caseworker Interviews

A semi-structured interview schedule was used to conduct interviews with caseworkers. The interview schedule captured basic demographic information about the qualifying adult offspring as well as brief description regarding the incidence of elder abuse and other forms of maltreatment by the adult offspring to the elder parent. Specific questions obtained information about: (1) the adult offspring at the time of the most recent abuse incident with respect to sex, race, age, marital status, employment status and annual income; (2) elder parent at the time of the most recent abuse incident with respect to sex, race, age, marital status, annual household income, living arrangements and family relationship to the adult offspring; (3) incidents of physical abuse with respect to date of the most recent incident, type of physical abuse for the most recent incident and number of abuse incidents; and (4) other forms of maltreatment. All related questions were closed-ended.

After the closed-ended questions were answered, caseworkers were given an open-ended one on the dynamics of the abuse between adult offspring and elder parent. Specifically, they were asked to describe the relationship between the adult offspring and elder parent as well as their assessment of the cause for the abuse. The overall purpose of the caseworker interview was to capture information on all qualifying adult offspring in order to have (1) a general understanding of the group, (2) a basis of comparing those interviewed with qualifying adult offspring not interviewed in order to know whether or not the interviewed sample was representative of the whole, and (3) a source for verifying certain information obtained through questioning of the interviewed sample.

When background data had been obtained on a qualifying adult offspring, the caseworker was asked for an assessment of the availability and appropriateness of the individual for interview. Implications of this assessment were discussed between the caseworker and myself before a decision was made on whether or not to approach the adult offspring about being interviewed.

Interviews with caseworkers were conducted either by telephone or in person, usually in the caseworker's office. Between 10 and 25 minutes were required for completion of the caseworker interview surrounding each qualifying adult offspring. Information was obtained on a total of 40 qualifying adult offspring.

Adult Offspring Interviews

Semi-structured, focused interview schedules were used to conduct interviews with adult offspring. The first interview schedule had six sections, addressing demographic characteristics, pathology, social isolation, stress and family conflict of the adult offspring along with vulnerability and other characteristics of the elder parent. The second interview schedule had three sections, addressing living or being with the elder parent, perception of social support and individual problems. Multiple interviews were used in order to enhance the depth and validity of information obtained.

Immediately following each interview with the research subjects, the interviewer wrote field notes on the conditions of the interview. These notes included information on the specific location of the interview, persons present and their participation, appearance of the respondent and house (if applicable), atmosphere (e.g., household tension), interaction between the respondent and elder parent (if any), difficulties in interviewing and length of time of the interview.

Each qualifying adult offspring who agreed to be interviewed was seen on two different occasions. Between 14 and 84 days. (M 55.7 days, SD 21.014) separated the first interview from the second. The first interview averaged 140 minutes (SD 84.028), the second 84.6 minutes (SD 55.069).

The vast majority of the interviews occurred in the respondent's residence (80.0% first interview, 85.7% second interview). Only rarely did they occur in the interviewer's residence, caseworker's office or a commercial setting. Usually no one else was present during the interview (60.0% first interview, 85.7% second interview). When others were present, they generally were the elder parent or other family members. Every subject, however, was interviewed alone at least some time.

The first interview with a subject occurred as soon as it could be arranged following the receipt of the subject's identity by the caseworker. It began with explaining the study and obtaining informed consent to participate. The second interview began by differentiating the content of this interview from the first and restating the protections accorded the subject around response anonymity and confidentiality. During the course of both interviews responses to questions were recorded, and extraneous remarks made by respondents were indicated. In addition, probing for clarification or elaboration of responses was done whenever appropriate and the responses recorded in the blank areas on the instruments near related questions. Exact quotes were taken as much as possible.

Respondents received ten dollars for each interview in which they participated. Payment was made to compensate respondents for the time they gave to the study, which in some instances was considerable. In addition, for a few subjects, the payment was probably an incentive for participation. Only one respondent did not accept the ten dollar payment.

Of the 40 qualifying adult offspring, 15 completed the first interview and 14 also the second interview. One subject was not willing to be interviewed a second time, because his elder parent died the week the request for interview was made. He felt he could "no longer talk about the situation" as a result.

Among those qualifying adult offspring who were not interviewed, most were unavailable (n = 14, 35.0% of the total) or inappropriate (n = 8, 20.0%) for interview. Only three (7.5%) refused to be interviewed, because they did not want to be bothered or because they felt the interview would be upsetting. The usual reasons for unavailability were because the whereabouts of the adult offspring were unknown (n = 8, 57.1% of those unavailable for interview) or because the adult offspring would not permit outside intervention or contact (n = 3, 21.4%). The reasons for inappropriateness for interview were near equally because (1) the adult offspring's pathology rendered her or him incapable of being interviewed (n = 3, 37.5% of those inappropriate for interview), (2) the adult offspring or other household member posed a danger to the elder parent or interviewer if the interview was conducted (n = 3, 37.5%), and (3) the interview would adversely affect present case planning (n = 2, 25.0%).

By and large, the research subjects readily answered interview questions and freely dicussed their relationship with the elder parent. Only twice did subjects refuse to answer specific questions, once with respect to annual income and once with respect to history of child abuse. In the former instance the matter was regarded as private, in the latter too upsetting for further explanation. Only one subject had difficulty understanding any specific questions. In this case, the subject's mental retardation rendered him unable to comprehend two open-ended questions on the second interview schedule. These particular questions required a greater ability to abstract than the subject possessed.

Extensive elaboration of particular topics, when it occurred, more reflected idiosyncrasy on the part of individual subjects than any other factor. For many, the interviews seemed almost cathartic in providing subjects with an opportunity to describe for a willing listener the problems, pain, and sometimes even pleasure, involved in caring for and interacting with the elder parent. It was from this need that many interviews lasted so long. When there were reservations about specific questions, they were related to recent abuse of the elder parent, and took the form of giving misinformation (at least in comparison with information obtained through interview with the caseworkers), probably out of a desire to "save face." However, even here, many subjects were quite open and detailed in describing the abuse, even when the abuse was severe and repeated.

First Interview Schedule

The first interview schedule, like the others used in this study, was constructed specifically for use in this investigation. It was developed to meet certain criteria. First, the interview schedule had to provide indicators for the various constructs that made up the conceptual framework.

Second, the organization and content of the first interview schedule had to be perceived as nonthreatening. It was assumed that many subjects would approach questions regarding elder care and family conflict with suspicion and misgiving. In most cases, the situation of abuse involving themselves and the elder parent had been reported to local authorities who had responded under legal mandate by investigating the report and attempting to provide intervention toward preventing further abuse occurrence. Because the report and investigation had the perceived effect of calling into question the quality of care provided the elder parent by the adult offspring at best, or the morality of the adult offspring's behavior toward the elder parent at worst, it seemed likely that some subjects would be defensive during interviews, and questioning therefore would need to proceed with caution.

Third, the interview schedule had to be written in clear, simple language. Moreover, the format for its administration had to be easy to understand. Not only was it likely that a wide range of intellectual and educational levels would be represented among the respondents, it was also possible that the interview schedule would be used by other interviewers than myself. Initially one referral source had agreed to participate in the study only if its caseworkers conducted the interviews. Although this requirement was rescinded before the onset of data collection, one caseworker wanted to interview at least one respondent, and it was arranged for him to be trained and supervised for this purpose.

Fourth, the interview schedule had to provide respondents with an opportunity to elaborate when they wished. Given the usual perceived difficulties involved in filial caregiving and the need to "unload" emotions surrounding it, an assumption was made that respondents would require both structured and unstructured opportunities to do so.

The interview went through numerous revisions. Input was initially received from Jill Korbin and Kevin Eckert of Case Western Reserve University's Department of Anthropology. As principal investigators of the National Institute on Aging funded research project, for which this study will serve as a pilot, they made suggestions around the general content and format of the interview schedule and reviewed the first draft. The second draft was reviewed by colleagues in the fields of aging and adult protective services as well as by Richard Gelles, nationally recognized authority on family violence, the latter upon request by Jill Korbin.

The third draft of the first interview schedule was pretested by five adult offspring who provided care to an elder parent but had no known history of elder abuse. The pretest group was obtained from the study's referral sources. It was purposively selected. An attempt was made to obtain a group diverse with respect to age, race, income, education, level of impairment of the elder parent and known quality of relationship with the elder parent. An attempt was also made to include in the pretest group those who might be difficult to interview by virtue of being unresponsive, suspicious, talkative or argumentative. Interviews were conducted in the respondent's residence or office. Members of the pretest group were each paid ten dollars for being interviewed.

The fourth draft of the first interview schedule was pretested (only for revisions from the third draft) by two colleagues in adult protective services. The fifth draft was the one used in the study. Piloting the instrument in this manner resulted in some questions being added, some eliminated, and the wording of a few changed.

The first interview schedule, like the second, was administered by myself and in one instance by a caseworker from a referral source. The other interviewer was trained for the task through (1) written instructions on completing the interview schedule, (2) verbal explanation of these instructions, and (3) role play on the administration of the instrument. In addition, we met after each interview he conducted to debrief. The other interviewer had an appropriate background for the task, having a psychology major at college and several years of work experience in counseling and providing other human services. There was never any reason to believe that his interviewing techniques or the responses he obtained from the subject he interviewed were substantively different than mine.

Second Interview Schedule

The purpose of the second interview was to explore in greater depth the meaning and dimensions of those variables found salient through initial interviewing. The second interview schedule reflected this purpose by limiting its scope and addressing only three major factors.

In addition to most of the criteria used to develop the first interview schedule, two criteria were important in constructing the second. First, the second interview schedule had to be shorter than the first. In order to address the various constructs of the conceptual framework, the first interview schedule required over two hours to administer. Coupled with the fact that most respondents also wanted to talk in general terms about their relationship with the elder parent, this meant that many first interviews were rather long, up to over six hours. As a result, there was a need to shorten the second interview in order to retain subject interest and cooperation.

Second, the second interview schedule had to be constructed to capture information on the salient variables at the same time that it did not appear to duplicate topics already covered by some respondents as extraneous remarks during the first interview. It generally succeeded at this. Only one respondent expressed displeasure at being asked a question the second round on a topic upon which she had commented the first round. When this happened, I simply acknowledged the fact and indicated that since the questions were designed for a large group and many members of that group had not commented on the topic, would not she bear with the repetition for the few questions that applied. She did, and the interview was completed without further expressed concern.

The second interview schedule was developed after analyzing the responses of the first eleven subjects interviewed using the first interview schedule. Salient variables were identified which served as the basis for the construction of specific questions for the second interview schedule. The initial draft was reviewed by colleagues in aging and adult protective services. The second draft was pretested by two members of the original pretest group. The particular individuals selected were those who represented the greatest contrast with respect to the original criteria of interest. Each was paid ten dollars for the interview. The third draft was used to interview the research subjects.

Special Appalachian Interview Schedule

After analyzing the results of the first eleven interviews, it became evident that some of the responses of one subject were categorically different in important respects from those of the other subjects. Most especially, she alone spoke in an easy, accepting manner about abusing her elder parent, e.g., "I change her and she does it again. I don't really get mad at her, but I tell her I'll spank her if she don't stop," and "I'd like to turn her upside down and spank her; I have a temper." It seemed possible that her Appalachian background had a role in explaining this quality. Therefore, a special Appalachian interview schedule was developed and administered by me to two purposively selected representatives of that culture obtained through the study's referral sources. The interview schedule was reviewed by colleagues who had worked with Appalachians on Cleveland's Near West Side. The Appalachian subjects were selected on the basis of four criteria: (1) middle-aged or older, (2) born and raised in an Appalachian state, (3) with parents who were born and raised in an Appalachian state, and (4) with a father who had worked in farming, mining, crafts or industry. Because these were thought to be shorter interviews, Appalachian subjects were compensated five dollars for their time. Interviews averaged 82 minutes and took place in the subject's residence or work setting.

Respondent Protections

Because the research subjects might have been at risk of emotional distress and identification of further elder abuse during the interviews, special protective measures were taken. At the close of each interview session, the subject was given a card on which was typed the name and telephone number of the referral source. The interviewer then urged the subject to contact the referral source if any help was needed around problems with the elder parent or as a result of the interview. In addition, the letter of informed consent contained an underlined statement that cautioned the subject that any information given on current maltreatment of an elder under Ohio law would be reported to the local county department of human services. In fact, at the end of one interview, the subject encouraged me to report the possibility of further abuse to her mother to the county department of human services. After counseling her on the matter, we agreed that a more appropriate initial step would be for her to reenter therapy around the long term relationship issues that generated conflict between her and the mother. She did this, and no report was made.

Other, more typical, research subject protections included the following: (1) No interviews were conducted without a signed letter of informed consent. (2) Subjects were assured that they could refuse to answer any question or withdraw from the interview at any point without adverse consequence. (3) Subjects were assigned an identification number, and all interview schedules and other records were identified on the basis of this number alone. Only I held the name-identification number code, and this was kept in a locked file until the completion of the data collection phase, when it was destroyed.

HANDLING THREATS TO VALIDITY

Many threats to internal and external validity were controlled through this research design. With regard to history, for example, events could have occurred between the administration of the first interview schedule and the second which altered the perception of social support from that indicated during the first interview. To illustrate, the research subject's base of social support may have changed as a result of the departure of her or his closest friend. Because the event occurred subsequent to administration of the first interview schedule, it would not have been evident in responses to questions in the social isolation section, and yet it may have affected the subject's perception of social support. It was anticipated that the wording of items in the perception of social support section of the second interview schedule would capture some related information, however. The questions were phrased so that events such as a best friend's death or moving away could be noted. In addition, the questions were broad enough to elicit multiple sources of perceived support or isolation.

Mortality could have resulted if some caseworkers or adult offspring were unwilling to complete the interviews. Nonetheless, the interviews were fairly interesting and generally nonthreatening. They also related to topics caseworkers and adult offspring usually like to discuss, otherwise why the prevalence of team case conferences in adult protective services and support groups among filial caregivers.

The potential threat of instrumentation was addressed by having the same interviewer for each interview with a research subject, and using the same set of instructions for interview schedule administration.

Testing may have been a problem, since the interviewed sample was twice interviewed. However, this threat was diminished through the use of different questions during each interview. Selection bias was also not a threat, except as noted elsewhere. This was because all qualifying adult offspring were included in the investigation, and all those available, appropriate and willing to be interviewed were included in the interviewed sample. There was no differential selection.

Maturation may have been a concern as subjects became more burdened by caregiving or angrier at the elder parent from the first interview to the second. The effect on research findings should have been minimal, however, because domains of inquiry differed by interview. Finally, the reactive or interaction effect of testing may have threatened external validity. Completion of the first interview schedule could have affected the behavior of adult offspring, including making them more suspicious, for instance, which in turn may have influenced the results from the second interview. The time lapse between interviews should have helped offset any possible effect. In addition, because the various measures were distinctive, they should have had little impact on one another.

MEASUREMENT

Caseworker Interview Schedule

Besides providing overall demographic data on the qualifying adult offspring and their elder parents from the perspective of the referral source caseworkers, this interview schedule measured the physical abuse of the elder parent. Caseworkers were asked the nature of abuse incidents that had been substantiated according to the criteria of this study and which qualified the adult offspring for inclusion in the study. Their descriptions contained the date of the most recent incident and type of physical abuse for the most recent incident.

Coding for type of physical abuse followed the modified version of the Violence Scale of the Conflict Tactics Scale described later in this chapter. That for other maltreatment forms duplicated coding employed by Sengstock and Liang (1982) in their elder abuse research. Coding for most other items of this instrument reflected standard categories found in the literature, e.g., white, black, Hispanic, Asian, and other for race.

First Interview Schedule

The first interview schedule was constructed to elicit information which would measure variables of constructs comprising the conceptual framework, including history of family violence, pathology, stress and social isolation for the adult offspring and vulnerability for the elder parent. Demographic characteristics for the adult offspring were also obtained from this source.

Demographic Characteristics

The first section of the interview schedule attempted to establish the demographic characteristics of the research subjects. The information sought, and so the variable name, can be easily comprehended from the wording used for each related question, e.g., "What is your marital status?" The variables for which information was sought surrounded sex, race, marital status, age, religion, nationality, schooling, employment status, and income source and amount. Most of these questions were closed-ended. Coding followed standard formats, e.g., U.S. Bureau of the Census categories for occupation. Subjects were advised that "don't know" was a valid response throughout the interview.

Pathology

The second section of the interview schedule measured the pathology of the subjects, primarily during the last two years. The time period of reference throughout both interviews was the last two years. This particular period was selected, because during this time all incidents of elder abuse occurred which qualified the subjects for inclusion in the study. Two years was also thought to represent an outside limit for subject recall of the detail required to answer the questions posed during interviews.

The initial items in this section asked the subjects to rate their overall physical health and overall mental health using a four-point Likert-type scale, and then identify any recent health problems. Likert-type scaling was used to measure health status, and other research variables in this study, because it tends to be easy to construct, reliable, and able to generate more precise information than dichotomous responses can provide. The limitations of Likert-type scaling were also recognized, e.g., subjects sometimes gravitate to certain responses, but were found outweighed by the advantages of this kind of scaling.

Health-related items were followed by closed-ended questions on hospitalization for emotional health problems, drinking of alcoholic beverages, and use of drugs to speed up or slow down. Depending on the responses made to these questions, further information was sought using open-ended questions on such topics as the diagnosis with hospitalization; type, quantity and frequency of alcoholic beverages consumed; and perception of having a substance abuse problem. The variables tapped in this section were physical illness, diagnosed mental illness, undiagnosed emotional distress, and alcohol and other drug abuse.

Vulnerability

By and large, the third section of the first interview schedule addressed characteristics which diminished the elder parent's capacity to resist or retaliate against abuse occurrence. Specifically, subjects were asked to rate the elder parent's overall physical and emotional health status, again using a four-point Likert-type scale. Additional questions sought an identification of health problems and their perceived effect on the elder parent's functioning. Subjects were also asked the living arrangements of the elder parent during the last two years in order to consider issues of proximity and potential dependency between the elder parent and adult offspring.

Two questions which sought general information about the elder parent were added to this section after pretesting the instrument. Pretesting revealed that filial caregivers had a need early in the course of being interviewed to simply "talk about" the elder parent. Subjects were permitted to do this by giving the elder parent's age and then describing the elder parent in terms of personality and interests. The items in the third section were a mixture of open-ended and closed-ended questions.

Social Isolation

The fourth section of the first interview schedule concerned the social isolation of the research subjects. It was divided into five parts. The first part measured frequency of contact with others, both those within the subjects' informal network (e.g., relatives, neighbors) and those within their formal network (e.g., clergy, doctor). Part two addressed the social activities of the subjects during the last two years, seeking responses on frequency of participation and associates for specified activities. The third part was included in an attempt to discover what help the subjects recently received from other persons. Related questions measured type and frequency of help received and categories of helpers. Part four considered the kind of formal activities undertaken by subjects during the last two years as well as the frequency with which they were undertaken. Most of the questions in the first four parts of this section required both closed-ended and open-ended responses.

Finally, the last part of the fourth section of the first interview schedule focused on the subjects' perception of social support. Using four-point Likert-type scaling, these items explored such dimensions of social support as feelings of intimacy and confidence to receive assistance when needed. The seven items in this part formed the Social Isolation Index, an index developed for this study. Potential scores ranged from 7 to 28, with higher ones indicating greater perceived social isolation. The scores for certain items were reversed to calculate the final score. Chronbach's alpha for the index was .79. Content validity for the index was derived from the item sources, i.e., the literature on social support and review by human service providers.

Stress

The fifth section of the first interview schedule measured stress experienced by the research subjects during the last two years. Part one specifically related to stress internal to the caregiving relationship, part two to life crisis events.

The initial set of internal stress questions consisted of a 28-item listing of types of care that might be performed for an elder. It was taken from the Benjamin Rose Institute's (1980) Family Assessment of Caregiving to Seniors (FACTS). For each item, the subjects were asked the following: (1) Was the task performed (closed-ended question)? (2) If so, how often (open-ended)? (3) Was it bothersome (Likert-type scale)? (4) How often was help provided (open-ended)?

The next set of internal stress questions addressed burden of caregiving. Within that set, open-ended questions concerned how family decisions were made around caring for the elder parent, perception of the elder parent's feelings as recipient of that care, and perception of the distribution of family caregiving responsibilities as fair. Closed-ended questions within that set measured the burden of providing care to the elder parent, using questions which represented a modification of the Zarit Burden Inventory (Zarit et al, 1980) and four-point Likert-type scaling. The wording of items in this inventory was changed to make them easier to understand and more acceptable to the subjects of the study. In addition, items were added to address other dimensions of caregiving and perceived burden. Composite scores for the Burden of Elder Caregiving Index suggested degree of perceived burden in caring for the elder parent, with higher scores indicating greater perceived burden than lower scores. The scoring for certain items was reversed in calculating the composite scores. The final index had a Chronbach's alpha coefficient of .87. One item had been dropped from the original index because of poor intercorrelations with other items and the total score. There was not much variability among the responses to this item.

The final set of internal stress questions identified behaviors of the elder parent that the subjects might find disturbing, and asked the subjects to reveal: (1) whether or not the elder parent had behaved in this way during the last two years (closed-ended question); (2) if so, an illustration of when this happened (open-ended); and (3) the subject's usual response when the elder parent behaved in this way (open-ended). The last of this series of questions was asked in part to determine if specific disturbing behaviors of the elder parent triggered abuse by the subjects. Disturbing behaviors identified included refusing to do what was asked, creating a mess, and complaining or criticizing. The sources for the identification of disturbing behaviors used in this set of questions, i.e., the literature on caregiving and review by colleagues in the field of aging, provided content validity for those selected.

Questions on external stress originated with the Holmes and Rahe (1967) Social Readjustment Rating Scale as modified by Straus and Gelles for the National Family Violence Study (Straus, 1980b). The scale addressed stressful life events. Unlike the original, the Straus and Gelles version considered only the negative events. Gerstein et al (1974) and Paykel (1974) have shown that the negative items account for most of the relationship between stress index scores and other variables.

A final item in this section required the subjects to provide overall assessment of their state of happiness during the last two years and account for that state in specific ways. It was included to determine the extent to which the elder parent was perceived as coloring the subjects' overall state of mind.

History of Family Violence

The last section of the first interview schedule dealt with the subjects' past history of observing or participating in family violence. Part one in this section explored that history during the subjects' childhood. It began with a set of questions, mostly open-ended, which asked the subjects to describe child discipline techniques used by their parents and how their parents behaved with each other when angry. It also included questions asking the subjects to identify any adult relatives with whom they had problems or particularly good relations when growing up, and why. These latter questions were included to learn if any history of family violence originated from a source other than the subjects' parents. The questions reveal a characteristic of item sets used in all instruments of this study. Whenever there are negatively-charged items in a set, at least one positively-charged item is included in order to render the item set more acceptable to respondents and better able to measure the breadth of meaning subjects associate with the variables under consideration.

Part one of the final section of the interview schedule concluded with a modified version of the 19-item Conflict Tactics Scale. This scale was designed and used by Straus et al (1980) for measuring violence between spouses, parents and children, and siblings. It has become a widely used and accepted measure of the ways family members settle differences among themselves. It presents various tactics for settling differences, and asks subjects to indicate how often, if ever, the tactics are used, and by whom. Three different types of tactics are measured: reasoning, verbal or symbolic aggression, and violence (meaning the use of physical force). The last eight items represent the Violence Scale; they begin with "threw something at the other one" and end with "used a knife or gun."

In the modified version of the Conflict Tactics Scale, which I developed for this study, particular conflict tactics were added that are more peculiar to elderly victims. This was important, since the scale was used for measuring violence in part two of this section, which represented the last two years and targeted interaction between the subjects and the elder parent. Items that were added included "restrained the other as punishment," "forced the other to use drugs or alcohol," and "choked or tried to choke the other." The addition of such items resulted after review of numerous case examples of elder abuse found in the literature and discussions on the subject with colleagues in adult protective services.

Part one of the final section of the first interview schedule addressed the use of conflict tactics between the subjects and their parents during childhood, part two between the subjects and their elder parent during the last two years. The internal consistency reliability of the original Conflict Tactics Scale ranged between .82 and .87 for various composite indices (Straus et al, 1980). That obtained for the modified version used in this study was .68. The only item that could have been dropped to increase the reliability coefficient was "got information to back up (your/ her or his) side of things," an item included in the original Conflict Tactics Scale. The item was not dropped in order to retain the entirety of a scale so widely used in family violence research and therefore conceptually important in understanding elder abuse as one aspect.

Throughout the first interview schedule, at the end of each set of questions around a topic, there occurred an open-ended question which gave subjects an opportunity to add something of their own not covered in the set. For example, at the conclusion of questions on the subjects' formal network, the following questions were asked: "Are there any persons, other than the ones I've named, that you talked with about problems or personal matters during the last two years? (If 'yes') Who are these persons?" In addition, at the end of the first interview, as well as the second interview, subjects were asked if they had any further comments to make regarding caring for or being around the elder parent. This was done to provide respondents with the fullest possible opportunity to relate words and with respect to all those dimensions they considered important. Any remarks made were recorded on the last page of the interview schedule.

Finally, the particular ordering of the various sections of the first interview schedule and the sequencing of questions within each section reflected an attempt to make the interview less threatening to subjects and therefore better able to elicit their honest perceptions on all matters addressed.

Second Interview Schedule

As stated earlier, after the first interview schedule had been administered to eleven research subjects, the results were analyzed and a second interview schedule developed to explore in greater depth those variables found most salient for explaining elder abuse. Analysis of data at this stage consisted of calculating frequencies and descriptive statistics for closed-ended questions. The content analysis of open-ended questions, as well as extraneous remarks, resulted in the development of related coding schemes, which in turn were subjected to descriptive statistical analysis.

The profile of the abusing adult offspring that emerged from preliminary analysis suggested a white, unmarried Catholic, either working for pay or functioning as a homemaker, and complaining of recent physical health problems and fair to poor emotional health. She or he resided with the elder parent, who was of advanced old age and perceived as having fair or poor physical and emotional health. The adult offspring gave indication of individual pathology but not stress or history of family violence. She or he had regular contact with friends, relatives and neighbors; recently discussed problems or personal matters with a counselor and physician; and received a good deal of help from her or his social network. However, the adult offspring felt a lack of social support. In addition, the adult offspring tended to be an only child, only unmarried child, or only child residing in the vicinity of the elder parent. She or he was either economically dependent on the elder parent, or there were allegations that she or he may financially abuse the elder parent. The adult offspring found the elder parent demanding and unwilling to do what was expected around the receipt of care. Moreover, she or he did not see the family as doing its fair share of providing care to the elder parent.

Each of the above characteristics described at least seven of the eleven subjects. Particularly strong trends were noted with respect to three of these characteristics, i.e., indication of individual pathology, residence with the elder parent, and perceived lack of social support. Each of these characteristics was suggested for at least ten of the eleven subjects. On this basis, it was decided that the second interview schedule would examine these three variables in greater depth. Accordingly, the purpose of the second interview schedule was to answer the following questions: (1) Were there dynamics associated with living with an elder parent that contributed to abuse occurrence? If so, what were they? What factors kept the adult offspring and elder parent in residence together? (2) Under circumstances of having regular contact with a social network and receipt of help when needed, what accounted for perceived social isolation? Did this perception relate to particular social deficiencies or general feeling? (3) What were the symptoms of emotional distress or individual pathology experienced by subjects? Which symptoms were seen as resulting from being around the elder parent?

Given the purpose of the second interview schedule, it was divided into three sections. The first section dealt with living with the elder parent (or being with the elder parent in those couple instances where the subject did not actually reside with the elder parent). Questions in part one of this section measured the period of residence together since the adult offspring was age 18 years and during the last two years (closed-ended questions), as well as general perception of residence with the elder parent and identification of things the elder parent did to make living together easier or harder (combination of closed- and open-ended questions). Part two determined whether or not the subjects had considered or would consider alternative living arrangements for the elder parent, and if so, under what circumstances and which alternative living arrangements (combination of closed- and open-ended questions).

Part three of the first section consisted of a 11-item index for measuring feelings associated with intimacy with an elder parent. The index was constructed for the present research and labeled the Social Intimacy Index. Selection of items was based on the range of possible emotions associated with residence or being together, with emphasis on those that suggested ill-feeling, conflict or abuse. The list of items was developed from three sources: (1) comments made by the pretest group for the present study, (2) discussions with colleagues in human services, and (3) the literature on stresses and burdens of elder caregiving (e.g., Schmidt, 1980; Miller, 1981; Springer & Brubaker, 1984). This method of identifying feelings provided content validity for the items selected. Each of the items was given equal weight. Four-point Likert-type scaling was used to score responses. The total score represented the respondent's feeling regarding living with the elder parent. Low scores suggested negative feelings, high scores positive feelings. The scoring on certain items had to be reversed in computing the total score. The Cronbach's alpha coefficient for the index was .74

Part four of the first section allowed respondents to describe in their own words what it was like being around the elder parent during the last two years. This was done by the interviewer making incomplete statements about the elder parent or interaction with the elder parent. The subjects then were asked to complete the statements considering their related feelings. Examples of these statements include, "My (elder parent) is like a child when. . ." and "I get angry with my (elder parent) when. . .". The items in this part were developed from the extraneous remarks made by the subjects during the first interview. Those remarks that related to intimacy or residence with the elder parent and showed promise for providing greater meaning to this variable were developed into statements for use in this part of the instrument.

The second section of the second interview schedule assessed perception of social support. In so doing, it explored the meaning of good friendship, family and good neighbors for the subjects through specific consideration of close individual relations. In addition, qualities that might be missing in these relations which render them less than desirable were addressed. Another set of questions explored occasions during the last two years when someone lifted up or let down the subjects, especially as related to the elder parent. Finally, other questions measured the effect of current marital status on ability to care for the elder parent. Section two of this interview schedule was mainly comprised of open-ended questions.

The third, and final, section of the second interview schedule assessed problems experienced by the subjects during the last two years that might indicate pathology, or might give fuller meaning to the emotional distress acknowledged by respondents during the first interview. Four-point Likert-type scaling was used to measure each of 29 problems listed. Scoring reflected the frequency with which identified problems were experienced, if at all, during the period in question. The list of problems was largely derived from the Psychiatric Status Schedule (Spitzer et al, 1970), and notably these sections which evaluate subjective distress. Identified problems included "worried a lot," "felt angry a lot," and "regretted a great deal." Following the list of 29 items, subjects were asked if they had experienced other problems of everyday life during the last two years; if so, what problems; and among all problems experienced, which, if any, did they feel were as a result of being around the elder parent.

Special Appalachian Interview Schedule

The function of the special Appalachian interview schedule was to measure the use and acceptance of violence to resolve conflict in Appalachian culture, particularly within the context of family, between adults, and against elders. The first section of the instrument established the respondents' qualifications for completing the interview. In other words, questions were asked which assessed the respondents' background with regard to state of birth, length of residence outside Appalachia, state of birth for both parents and occupation of father. The second section of the interview schedule addressed the discipline used on the respondents as children and how their parents behaved when angry with each other. The wording of questions in this section paralleled that found in the last section of the first interview schedule. Section three (combination of closed- and open-ended questions) asked respondents to reveal if they had seen specific violent acts between adults when growing up, and if so, to identify the parties involved, how often the acts occurred, and their related feelings. The list of acts represented the Violence Scale of the Conflict Tactics Scale as modifed for this study and used in the first interview schedule. Section four (combination of closed- and open-ended questions) assessed whether or not the respondents or their friends caused physical pain or injury to another person when growing up, and if so, the nature of the violence. The fifth section consisted of four statements that subjects completed based on their understanding of life in Appalachia. The intent of this section was to provide subjects with an opportunity to express in their own words Appalachian norms around (1) the treatment of elders, (2) manhood, (3) family, and (4) acceptable violence. Finally, the last section of the special Appalachian interview schedule focused directly on elder abuse in Appalachia by using open-ended questions to assess incidents of abuse observed by the respondents and expectations around elder abuse in Appalachia.

CHAPTER IV

PRESENTATION AND DISCUSSION
OF FINDINGS

INTRODUCTION

THIS CHAPTER presents the results of data analysis, beginning with the techniques used for the task. Thereafter, the characteristics of the qualifying adult offspring are described from information obtained from referral source caseworkers. Next, the characteristics of the interviewed sample are detailed as they emerged from repeated interviews with the subjects. Characteristics in this regard include those specifically relevant to the conceptual framework of the study. Conflict in Appalachia is then described from interviews with selected representatives of this culture. The chapter concludes with a discussion of major findings.

DATA ANALYSIS

Data analysis was descriptive in form and sought to answer the research questions posed earlier. Accordingly, statistical procedures were limited to frequency counts and percentage distributions of descriptive variables and chi squares for a few relationships. The nature of purposive comparison and the small size of the interviewed sample were such that findings did not readily lend themselves to even advanced descriptive statistical techniques of analysis. Responses to open-ended questions and extraneous remarks made by the interviewed sample were content analyzed as were the abuse dynamics described by caseworkers for the research sample. Coding schemes were developed from this analysis. Whenever possible, data were reduced and indices formed to facilitate description of the interviewed sample and the variable suggesting abuse etiology.

QUALIFYING ADULT OFFSPRING
SAMPLE DESCRIPTION

The total sample for the study was 40. This number represented all of the adult offspring known to the study's participating agencies and hospitals who qualified for inclusion in the research by having physically abused an elder parent during the last eighteen months. The vast majority of qualifying adult offspring had only recent contact with their referral source, the usual basis for that contact being reported abuse of the elder parent. This was to be expected. The primary referral sources for the study were county departments of human services (70 percent of all situations referred to the study originated from county departments of human services), and the usual reason for contact with agencies of this type, outside of receipt of income maintenance, relates to protective investigation and services.

Seventy-five percent of the sample had first contact with the referral source during the last 18 months, 20.0 percent prior to that time. For five percent there had never been contact with the referral source.

Nearly all of the qualifying adult offspring were white. Blacks constituted only five percent of the sample, and there were no Hispanics or Asians represented. With regard to sex, the sample was near equally divided. Most were middle-aged. Only 2.5 percent of the sample was under age 30, and 15.0 percent were 60 years and over. For five percent age was unknown. The majority were unmarried, mostly having never married (30.0%) or divorced (12.5%). Forty-five percent were either working for pay or as a homemaker. Most of the remaining were unemployed (32.5%). Annual income for the sample tended to be low, with 60.0 percent earning less than $15,000 per year. Only 7.5 percent had a reported annual income of $30,000 or more.

The abused elder parent represented through the research sample was characterized as a white, widowed woman of advanced old age living with her natural son or daughter who was the abuser. Almost 78.0 percent of the elder parents were female, 92.5 percent white, 55.0 percent age 80 or more, and 85.0 percent widowed. Ninety-five percent lived with the abused adult offspring, who in 80.0 percent of the situations was the natural son or daughter of the elder parent. Only rarely was the relationship that of step-child (5.0%) or in-law (12.5%). It should be noted that one qualifying adult offspring was neither son nor daughter on any basis to the elder parent. Although technically a grand-

child, he was included in the research sample, because the elder parent
had raised him since infancy, thereby duplicating a parent-child relationship. Seventy-five percent of the elder parents represented through
the sample had an annual income of less than $15,000.

The most recent incident of physical abuse of the elder parent by the
adult offspring tended to occur within six months of referral source contact with the study. This, I believe, reflected a tendency among most
participating agencies and hospitals not to maintain adequate records
for identifying abuse among their clients or patients. As a result, when
asked to review these records for referral to the study, caseworkers could
only identify abuse occurring in those situations they currently serve or
recently served. This obviously presents a sample bias for the study.
Those represented in the sample for the most part are current or recent
cases, or those wherein the abuse was severe or readily apparent and so
more frequently noted or remembered.

Abuse most often took the form of pushing, grabbing, shoving or
shaking (30.0%), although slapping or spanking (17.5%) and beating
up (17.5%) were also common abuse forms. Where it was known by the
caseworker, there usually had been many (7 +) incidents of abuse by the
adult offspring to the elder parent. In only ten percent of the situations
had abuse occurred but once or twice, and in only 17.5 percent of additional situations had it occurred a few (3-6) times. Other forms of
maltreatment also tended to be represented (75.0%), and generally took
the form of psychological abuse (52.5%), although physical neglect
(27.5%) and financial abuse (25.0%) were not uncommon.

Caseworkers ordinarily saw the reason for abuse occurrence on the
part of the adult offspring to be some form of individual pathology,
whether unstable personality (32.5%), unresolved family conflict
(30.0%), alcoholism (27.5%), mental illness (27.5%), drug abuse
(12.5%), or mental retardation (10.0%). Stress (15.0%) and history of
family violence (7.5%) were much less frequently mentioned. The characteristics of the elder parent which were seen as contributing to abuse
occurrence were most often physical impairment (62.5%) or mental impairment (40.0%).

By and large, the profiles of the abusing adult offspring, elder parent
and abuse that emerged from this study based on information provided
by referral source caseworkers were comparable with the findings from
other elder abuse research.

With regard to the abusing adult offspring, the findings of this study
agreed with most others in describing the perpetrator as middle-aged

and living with the abuse victim (for a review of early research on elder abuse see Langley, 1981; Sengstock and Liang, 1982; Wolf et al, 1984). It differed with all but Sengstock and Liang, however, in discovering a near equal distribution between the sexes. Other investigations found the perpetrator more typically female (Lau and Kosberg, 1979; Block and Sinnott, 1979) or male (Chen et al, 1981; Wolf et al, 1984).

The findings from this study also compared with most other research on elder abuse in describing the usual victim as female and widowed (Langley, 1981; Chen et al, 1981; Wolf et al, 1984). They are consistent with the earliest research in portraying her as impaired and very old (Langley, 1981). They agreed with the most recent research in revealing a low annual income for the victim (Chen et al, 1981; Sengstock and Liang, 1982; Wolf et al, 1984).

The results of the present study were similar to those of Wolf et al (1984) with regard to the most common types of physical abuse. Beating up, however, was less frequent and having something thrown at the victim more frequent among Wolf et al's sample. Variation between the studies here may reflect differences in related questions rather than any other factor. Wolf et al asked victims whether or not the several abuse forms comprising the Violence Scale of the Conflict Tactics Scale had occurred to them. In contrast, this study asked caseworkers to identify only the most recent abuse incident, and responses made were coded using the modified version of this scale. It may be that other abuse incidents took other forms, and their frequencies resemble those uncovered by Wolf et al.

The presence of multiple forms of maltreatment was also a finding of the other elder abuse investigations as was the occurrence of multiple physical abuse incidents. In the former regard, for example, Lau and Kosberg (1979) noted the usual presence of more than one form of abuse, although physical abuse, broadly defined, was the most prevalent. Wolf et al (1984) found the usual case of elder abuse represented two types of abuse, ordinarily psychological abuse and some other type. Multiple abuse incidents were acknowledged from the research of Block and Sinnott (1979), O'Malley et al (1979), and Lau and Kosberg (1979), among others. Wolf et al (1984) noted the long length of time an elder victim had sustained abuse or neglect, an average of over 43 months. Narrowly focusing on physical abuse, they found that such abuse forms as pushing, grabbing or shoving along with slapping tended to happen more than once or twice, when they happened.

Finally, with respect to perceived cause of abuse, the results from interviewing referral source caseworkers for this study were most similar to those obtained by Wolf et al (1984), emphasizing individual pathology and deemphasizing such other possible etiologies as stress and history of family violence. There, however, was seen to be greater vulnerability contributing to abuse occurrence, at least in terms of impairment status, by caseworkers in this study than by the elder abuse victims in Wolf et al's research.

The particular profiles that emerged from analysis of information on the qualifying adult offspring may in part be interpreted as reflecting the general population of elderly persons and their adult offspring in American society. For example, it was not surprising that so few blacks, and other nonwhites, were represented as abuse victims, since their proportion of the aged population tends to be small. In Ohio blacks comprise only 7.2 percent of the population aged 65 years and older (Ohio Data User's Center, 1985).

It was likewise to be expected that qualifying adult offspring tended to be middle-aged, since an offspring of any parent 60 years old or more is likely to be between 20 and 40 years younger and therefore middle-aged. Also, widowhood is the usual marital status for women in old age, and the vast majority of widowed women of advanced old age tend to be low income (U.S. Senate Special Committee on Aging and American Association of Retired Persons, 1984), so it was not surprising that the elder parents in this study who were women had similar characteristics.

Finally, women tend to outnumber men in the general elderly population, although in a proportion less than suggested by this study's results (U.S. Senate Special Committee on Aging, 1985). One reason for the discrepancy may relate to the possible greater vulnerability of women to abuse by virture of the traditional socialization accorded American girls and women, especially of past generations, with its emphasis on submission, helplessness and dependency (Williams, 1977).

Findings more atypical for the populations represented were the unmarried state of most qualifying adult offspring, since adults, especially by the time they reach middle-age, are or have been married (U.S. Bureau of the Census, 1981); the large percentage unemployed among the adult offspring, since recent data from the Ohio Bureau of Employment Services (1985) show only 9.4 percent of adults unemployed in the state; and the residence together of adult offspring and elder parent, since normally few elderly persons live with their adult children, even in advanced old age (Schorr, 1980; U.S. Senate Special Committee on Aging and American Association of Retired Persons, 1984). It was not possible to find good comparison data among existing elder abuse research for the variables of marital status and employment status of abusing adult offspring, undoubtedly because none of the studies interviewed the perpetrators. On the other hand, as indicated earlier, most literature on the subject suggests that the victim and perpetrator live together. In Wolf et al's (1984) research on all abuse forms, coresidence was characteristic of over 70.0 percent of subjects at three investigation sites, with the average number of years in coresidence exceeding 20.

It was important to the study's findings to learn whether or not the interviewed sample was different from those qualifying adult offspring who refused to be interviewed or were judged unavailable or inappropriate for interview. If the interviewed sample was self-selected and therefore different, it would not be possible to generalize the findings from interviews with this group to the total research sample.

In order to determine if the interviewed sample and noninterviewed sample of qualifying adult offspring could have come from the same population, chi square was computed for each variable wherein there was an expected cell frequency of at least one (Runyon & Haber, 1977). Computed variables were sex, race and income for the adult offspring; sex, race and age for the elder parent; and certain suggested causes of abuse, i.e., drug abuse, mental illness, mental retardation, unstable personality, unresolved family conflict and stress for the adult offspring and physical impairment, mental impairment, aggression or provocation, uncooperation, passive personality and social isolation for the elder parent. No association was found significant at the conventional .05 level for interview status and any variable considered, suggesting that the interviewed sample and non-interviewed sample came from the same population.

INTERVIEWED SAMPLE DESCRIPTION

First Interview

The purpose of the first interview was to identify salient variables for explaining elder abuse by adult offspring from among the theoretical interrelationships suggested in the conceptual framework of this study. Closed- and open-ended questions were employed to elicit information from the interviewed sample of abuse perpetrators on their demographic characteristics, pathology, stress, social isolation and history of family violence as well as the vulnerability of the elder parent. In addition, inquiry was made on the nature of recent abuse between the adult offspring and elder parent.

The presentation of findings from the first interview was accomplished in two parts: (1) demographic characteristics of the interviewed sample, and (2) dimensions of explored explanations for abuse occurrence. The latter part usually had two sections, the first largely based on statistical analysis of responses to closed-ended questions and the second based on content analysis of responses to open-ended questions and extraneous remarks.

Demographic Characteristics

Among the fifteen subjects comprising the interviewed sample, there were more men (60.0%) than women. Nearly all were white (93.3%). Most were unmarried (66.7%), usually having never married (33.3%) or divorced (26.7%). For those who had once married or were currently married, the length of time in their present marital status averaged 15.8 years.

The median and mean age for the interviewed sample was 49 and 51 years respectively. Most subjects were Catholic (53.3%). A broad range of schooling was represented, from none or less than five years (6.7%) to more than four years of college (26.7%). The largest number, however, had completed their education after some high school (33.3%) or high school graduation (20.0%).

A vast majority of subjects worked for pay or as a homemaker, including one who helped operate a family business (73.3%). Among those currently or recently employed, most worked as an operator or laborer. Salary or wages represented the main income source for most of the subjects (60.0%), although for 20.0 percent the main source was some kind of government benefit. One subject had no income. Finally, annual household income showed wide distribution, from under $3,000 (6.7%) to $50,000 plus (13.3%), with the most common range categories for income being $6,000-9,999 (26.7%) and $20,000-29,999 (20.0%).

The demographic profile which emerged for the interviewed sample suggested a white, middle-aged man who was unmarried and had at least some high school education. He considered himself Catholic and worked for pay as an operator or laborer. Salary or wages constituted his main income source. His income approximated $15,000 to $20,000 per year.

The various characteristics comprising this profile were consistent with one another and with demographic profiles for Americans of this age cohort or job classification (Fuchs, 1983). The only inconsistent findings were the larger number of men than women and the much larger number of Catholics than Protestants or other religious preferences represented in the interviewed sample.

There are two possible explanations for the larger number of men than women in the sample. Some of the difference may be an artifact of the availability or appropriateness of male research subjects to be interviewed. Some, however, may result from a differential propensity by sex to be physically abusive. In examining the population compositions for the counties represented in this study, there were consistently found to be more women than men in the age cohorts 45-59 and 50-54 (Ohio Data User's Center, 1985). If men and women were equally likely to physically abuse an elder parent, it would seem that the sample would have more women than men as well. Since this was not the case, it may be that men are more physically abusive than women. If so, this would be consistent with sex gender socialization which encourages men to be more aggressive (Williams, 1977). It would also be consistent with the research of Sengstock and Liang (1982), which found sons were more likely than daughters to physically abuse elder parents.

The much larger number of Catholics represented in the interviewed sample may be explained in a couple ways. First, Northeast Ohio has a large number of Catholics because of its high concentration of immigrants from Catholic European countries (Pap 1973; Ohio Data User's Center, 1985; Foy & Avato, 1986). The interviewed sample, therefore, may simply reflect the dominant religion of the region. This would be consistent with the findings from the Massachusetts and Maine studies on elder abuse, wherein the religion of the represented victims reflected the dominant religion of the represented states (O'Malley et al, 1979; Block & Sinnott, 1979). However, in neither study was the dominance of one religion over others as great as it was in the present study. Second, it may be that some Catholic groups have more tolerance of family violence or elder abuse than do Protestants or Jews. This would be consistent with the concept of subculture influencing abuse socialization expressed in chapter two of this study. In this regard, a paper by Carroll (1975) has particular interest. The study applied cultural consistency theory to Mexican-American and Jewish ethnic groups. It concluded that differences in levels of family violence were linked to differences in emphasis on male dominance and pursuit of knowledge between the groups.

Pathology

When asked to rate their physical health status during the last two years, the interviewed sample most often described it as good (46.7%). Only one-third of the subjects considered it fair or poor, even though the majority had experienced some health problems or illnesses during that time (80.0%). The largest number of these problems or illnesses could be classified as chronic illnesses, with (33.3%) or without (13.3%) a disability.

In contrast to physical health status, emotional health status tended to be seen as fair or poor (66.7%). Most subjects also identified specific problems during the last two years which had affected their emotional health (66.7%), with the usual perceived origins of those problems being interaction with the elder parent (46.7%). Two subjects had been hospitalized for mental illness, one for psychosis and the other for neurotic disorder, although neither during the last two years.

Sixty percent of the interviewed sample consumed alcoholic beverages during the period in question, with 44.4 percent of that group having at least three drinks per occasion and one-third drinking everyday. Forty-four percent of drinkers had been told that they had a drinking problem, and 22.2 percent agreed with this assessment.

Only two subjects had taken drugs to speed up during the last two years. If drugs were taken, their purpose was to slow down or sleep. Forty percent of the subjects had taken drugs for this reason, and usually an antianxiety drug (26.7%). No one had been told or thought that they had a drug problem.

Responses to open-ended questions or extraneous remarks during this portion of the first interview suggested that a sizable number of interviewed sample experienced unresolved family conflict with the elder parent (46.7%), emotional distress or mental impairment (40.0%), or alcohol abuse (33.3%). In addition, one subject showed evidence of an abusive self-concept and another was unaccepting of role reversal with the elder parent.

Unresolved family conflict was suggested in comments that dredged up past words and actions of the elder parent and held them in particularly unfavorable light. Such comments were often repeated throughout the interview and included the impression that relations with the elder parent had not improved over time, perhaps never could improve. Unresolved family conflicts represented old wounds never healed. For some respondents this conflict began in childhood, e.g., "[My mother] was always a problem to me. . .I can't help that [she] gave birth to me, but I don't have to like her." For others, the conflict was more recent, although still long term, e.g., "My father blames me for the kids. He picks all the time." Some respondents were acutely aware of the conflict, e.g., "We have always had such a bad relationship" and "I see myself struggling with the same issues with my mother as I always have." A few even considered the conflict pathological in nature, e.g., "My relationship with my father was like a psychodrama."

Emotional distress or mental impairment was indicated in the description of impairment symptoms or the acknowledgment of diagnosed illness, e.g., "I'm on psychotropic drugs; I get paranoid about milk cartons if I don't take them" and "I have an anxiety problem; the doctor says I have a severe one." It was also suggested in the use of therapy for personal problems, e.g., "[I wanted to hurt] my mother but this is nothing new; I went through a lot of therapy on this." Often the elder parent was blamed for the emotional distress, e.g., "My relationship with my father created such mental problems" and "Dealing with my mom and her problems made me pretty unhappy."

Alcohol abuse was evident in remarks on the frequency and amount of drinking, as well as in the perception of problem drinking by the respondent or others, e.g., "I go to the bar everyday." "I've been drinking a lot lately; that's been my social life," and "Even when I'm sober, I'm called a drunk by my kids and father."

Finally, an abusive self-concept was seen in the following illustrative remark of one subject's behavior, "I tend to get mad and snap, and someone winds up in intensive care." Unacceptance of role reversal was evidenced by the subject who declared, "I was not nurtured as a child, and here I was being asked to nurture him."

Overall, pathology could be said to characterize 11 of the 15 subjects of the interviewed sample (73.3%). In all but one instance, the pathology was evident in responses to open-ended questions or extraneous remarks and usually responses to closed-ended questions as well. The one instance where it was not represented a subject who was obviously mentally retarded by his words and behavior, and diagnosed as such by the referral source. Pathology within the interviewed sample took the form of emotional distress (36.4% of the total characterized by pathology), diagnosed mental illness (27.3%), alcohol abuse (27.3%) and mental retardation (9.1%). Although emotional distress may seem less tangible as a category of pathology than the others, this does not mean that its symptoms were any less significant to those afflicted. In two instances, the subjects had spent years in therapy for anxiety or depression; in another, the subject committed suicide within a month following the second interview. For all subjects experiencing emotional distress, the perceived origins for the distress were in relations with the elder parent.

Stress

Questions in the stress portion of the first interview related to stress internal to the caregiving relationship and stress resulting from life crisis events. The largest number of questions addressed internal stress and considered the types of care provided to the elder parent, help received, burden of caregiving, attitude of the elder parent to the receipt of care, and disturbing behaviors on the part of the elder parent.

The subjects provided an average of 10.6 types of care to the elder parent sometime during the last two years. The smallest number of types of care provided by any subject was four (20.0% of the subjects), the largest number 21 (6.7%). All subjects ran errands for the elder parent. Additionally, they usually did the cleaning (86.7%), provided regular checks or supervision (73.3%), prepared or served meals (73.3%), did extra laundry (66.7%), helped with medicines (66.7%), arranged for services or care (66.7%), managed financial or legal affairs (60.0%), and provided transportation (53.3%). For only a few types of care did subjects receive any help (M 2.5, range 0-12). Notwithstanding, they seldom or never found the tasks bothersome. In addition, the few that some subjects did find bothersome did not show particular patterning by category, e.g., personal care, housekeeping. Lack of patterning also characterized the types of care for which subjects received help, except that if a task was found bothersome, it did not tend to be one for which help was received.

Subjects assumed caregiving responsibilities for the elder parent primarily because of the unavailability or unsuitability of other adult offspring to do so. Either the subject was an only child, only living child or only capable child (53.3%) or the elder parent's other children refused or were uninterested or unavailable (46.7%). When a second reason was given, which was not often, it was most frequently because other care arrangements had failed (20.0%) or to prevent institutionalization (13.3%).

By and large, other family members were not seen as assuming their fair share of the caregiving responsibilities for the elder parent (66.7%). When asked how things could be different in this regard, subjects often could not give any suggestions (40.0%), perhaps because without siblings to share caregiving responsibilities, few viable options seemed apparent. Those suggestions that were made emphasized other family members being more supportive of the subjects' caregiving role by criticizing less (20.0%), providing respite (20.0%) or assuming some of the caregiving tasks (20.0%)

Results from analyzing the Burden of Elder Caregiving Index for this study suggested that as a whole the interviewed sample felt a moderate amount of burden from caring for the elder parent. With a potential score range of 12-48, the subjects' actual scores extended from 14 to 44, with 24.4 and 28 representing the mean and median scores respectively.

The primary source of perceived burden was in feeling stressed between caring for the elder parent and meeting other responsibilities at home or work (66.7% of subjects felt this often or sometimes). Responses to other items in this index suggested that the subjects were frequently angry around the elder parent (86.7%), felt the need to get away (53.3%) and did not have enough time for themselves (53.3%). They also felt that their health and relations with other family members had suffered during the last two years because of involvement with the elder parent (53.3%). Notwithstanding, the subjects were glad to be caring for the elder parent (86.6%), and felt at ease in company with the elder parent (60.0%). Few had guilt about the amount of time given to the elder parent (26.7%). Moreover, most felt that the elder parent only asked for help really needed (60.0%).

The majority of the subjects found the elder parent accepting of the care extended (53.3%). On the other hand, most also noted a number of disturbing behaviors on the part of the elder parent. Nearly all subjects described the elder parent as demanding and complaining or criticizing (80.0%). Most also could cite instances during the last two years when the elder parent used embarrassing public behavior or refused to do what was asked (60.0%). Moreover, a sizable number of elder parents were found to have behaved aggressively on occasion (46.7%).

By the same token, subjects acknowledged more positive behaviors on the part of the elder parent, including thanking the adult offspring for help received (66.7%), offering to pay for that help (53.3%) and giving the adult offspring privacy when needed (53.3%). On the other hand, sometimes these behaviors were viewed with suspicion by the subjects, who considered ulterior motive behind them. For example, one subject illustrated the elder parent's thanking him for help received by saying, "He would kiss my hand." The subject found this behavior embarrassing and suggestive of "sexual perversion" on the part of the father.

The subjects expressed considerable depth of feeling in describing instances wherein the elder parent exhibited disturbing behavior. They also varied in their usual response to these behaviors. Overall, however, the most common responses could be classified as insulting or swearing at the older parent, or sulking or refusing to talk about the issue.

Violence did occasionally occur, especially as a response to demanding behavior by the elder parent. As one subject described it, "At first I'd try to explain, then we'd argue and fight. That's the problem with old people; you can't make them understand."

The interviewed sample could not be characterized as afflicted by stressful life events during the last two years. The number of stressor events per subject ranged from 0 to 9; the potential range was from 0 to 18. The mean and median number of events per subject were 2.3 and 2 respectively. Those events that had occurred tended to surround the death of someone close (40.0%), or serious problems with the behavior of a family member or in-law troubles (26.6% each). In the latter two regards, the usual person of reference was the elder parent.

The vast majority of subjects considered themselves very happy or sort of happy (73.3%). The usual stated reasons for this were the elder parent (26.7%), other family members (20.0%) or finances or material possessions (20.0%). This is an interesting finding, because among subjects describing themselves as sort of unhappy or very unhappy, the usual reasons were the elder parent (26.7%) or other family members (26.7%) as well. Indeed, this seeming contradiction in perception regarding the elder parent was found throughout the first interview, both among the sample as a whole and among the responses of individual subjects. To illustrate the latter, consider the following comments made by a single respondent at different times during the interview:

> I've always loved my mother, and I like taking care of people. . .You can imagine the conflict — money, care, time — in caring for my mother . . .My mother made me angry. She wouldn't sign into a nursing home. She wanted me to have the guilt. As it was, the caseworker did it.

From content analysis of responses to open-ended questions in the stress portion of the interview and related extraneous remarks, three patterns were noted for sizable numbers of subjects. Nearly half of the interviewed sample indicated that the elder parent interfered with their need for independence (53.3%), e.g., "I feel cheated [in having to take care of my mother]. I used to say to her, 'When you were about 50, you and pa were free. I'm not.' " Furthermore, about one-third of the interviewed sample indicated that they lacked sufficient income (40.0%) and sufficient respite (33.3%). Those subjects who claimed insufficient income ordinarily were dependent on the elder parent to meet most or all of their living expenses. On the one hand, the subjects seemed to find financial dependency acceptable, sometimes believing that it benefited the elder parent as well, e.g., "My mother needed a home, and I needed an income" and "If she stays with me, I feel she should help with expenses." On the other hand, there was also resentment regarding the dependency and the elder parent's reaction to it, e.g., "I could use more money, but I'm working on this" and "[We're always arguing] about money. [She asks] that I show her my indebtedness, that I stop charging."

A need for respite was most often seen in comments expressing desired relief from the caregiving situation or disappointment that other family members refused to assume some of the responsibilities borne by the adult offspring. In the former regard, it was said, "I made a commitment. The deal was, 'Dad, you can die here.' But I never got a vacation." In the latter regard, one respondent lamented, "My sister goes and comes as she wants. She never says, 'Hey I'll give you a break.' "

In summary, the interviewed sample was not stressed as a result of life crisis events. Although they provided considerable care to the elder parent, and without much help, they did not find this particularly bothersome. What was a burden surrounded: (1) disturbing behaviors on the part of the elder parent; (2) the unavailability or unwillingness of other family members to assume a greater role in caregiving, or in supporting the subjects for the care they provided to the elder parent; and (3) little time available for self and other responsibilities because of elder caregiving. Subjects generally like taking care of the elder parent, but because of those sources of burden listed above, they often felt anger and other negative emotions around the elder parent, occasionally expressing these as psychological or physical abuse.

Social Isolation

This portion of the first interview explored the social isolation of the interviewed sample. In so doing, it assessed the subject's informal and formal contacts, social activities, formal activities, personal assistance received, and perception of social isolation.

Most subjects lived in households of very small size, usually consisting of only the subject and elder parent (46.6%). The average household size was three persons. Pets were more commonly present than not (53.3%).

Contact outside the household was maintained on a regular basis with in-county relatives (60.0%), friends (80.0%) and neighbors (66.7%). Outside-of-county relations were less regularly seen. On an average, subjects had monthly contact with 1.9 in-county relatives, 1.1 outside-of-county relatives, 4.1 friends and 2.2 neighbors. Of six possible categories of informal contacts, including household members and pets, the typical subject had regular contact with four.

The interviewed sample also had contact during the last two years with an average of two categories of formal support, most commonly a social worker or counselor, often the caseworker from the referral source (66.7%), doctor (46.7%), lawyer (46.7%) or clergy (40.0%). Problems or personal matters were discussed with these persons, sometimes quite often and in relation to the elder parent. Over time these individuals often became important sources of support for the subjects. One respondent described the three nuns upon whom he relied for help as "the only friends I've got." Another called her hairdresser her "confidante."

Of eight categories of social activities, including "other," about which subjects were asked, the interviewed sample averaged participation in 4.7 activities during the last two years (range 1-7). Those activities most frequently acknowledged were movies and other entertainment (80.0%), eating at restaurants (73.3%), shopping (66.7%) and parties (60.0%). Frequency of participation in most activities tended to be minimal, less than a few (3-6) times per year. Furthermore, the subjects' usual associates tended to be household members or friends.

Participation in formal activities was less often for most subjects. Of six identified categories, including "other," subjects participated in an average of only 1.8 during the last two years (range 0-4), with religious services (66.7%) and club or organization meetings (40.0%) those most commonly acknowledged. Three subjects participated in no formal activities during the last two years, and an equal number indicated rather extensive involvement. In the latter regard, for example, one subject listed his involvements to include attending church services and volunteering in nearly a half dozen civic associations at least once weekly each. Even as we sat during the interview, he listened for a radio alert to take him to his next assignment as volunteer fire fighter. This high level of activism contrasted sharply with other subjects whose formal activity participation was nonexistent, and who even expressed a certain measure of disbelief that I would ask such a question as "Did you do any volunteer work during this time?"

All subjects had received some kind of personal assistance or remembrance during the last two years. An average of 5.9 categories of assistance out of a possible 11 were acknowledged by the interviewed sample (range 2-10). The most commonly identified were having a special occasion remembered (100.0%) along with someone listening to troubles (93.3%), performing household tasks (73.3%), providing transportation (66.7%) or offering advice (60.0%). The source of that assistance tended to vary by category of assistance, with, for instance, friends more often offering advice or listening to troubles (emotional support) and family more often helping with household tasks and giving or lending money (instrumental support).

In exploring the subjects' social isolation through the index of the same name, a number of seeming contradictions or contrasts became apparent. Whereas 80.0 percent of the subjects felt that they often or sometimes had enough friends, 73.3 percent felt lonely. Whereas most usually felt close to someone (60.0%), most also felt that they did not receive a lot of credit for the things that they did (66.7%). Finally, whereas the majority of subjects felt that there was usually someone willing to help when needed (66.7%), they still wanted to get out of the house more (73.3%) and felt that there were a lot of things that they missed doing (86.7%). Despite these seeming contradictions or contrasts, the median composite score on the index was 22, indicating a fairly high degree of perceived social isolation on the part of the interviewed sample (potential range 7-28, actual range 7-23, M 18.4, SD 5.779).

Likewise, content analysis of responses to open-ended questions and extraneous remarks for this portion of the interview suggested that a sizable number of subjects perceived a lack of adequate social support (46.7%). Although the source that felt deficiency was usually the extended family, occasionally it was friends or neighbors. In only two instances were multiple sources acknowledged. As one of these two social isolates described it, "My social life has always been a problem. I have never really mixed well. . .[My family] has reacted with indifference towards me. . .I have some friends who have disappointed me." He believed that various choices made over the years further inhibited him socially, including living with his mother and once having worked swing shift.

For other subjects the origin of their social isolation was different. One subject avoided social groups because of impairment from a stroke suffered years before. Another did not mix in the neighborhood, because it was "all colored." Still another felt her entire family had disappointed her in important ways. When she finished listing the family members and her disappointments with regard to each, the list included over a dozen persons and the theme of her disappointments throughout was embodied in her final statement, "None of my [family] contributed to her care. I have felt alone in taking care of my mother. . .They also don't acknowledge how difficult it has been for me with my mother. Actually, it's been like a two-year funeral."

Generally speaking, the interviewed sample could be described as having had many informal and formal network contacts and a moderate amount of participation in social and formal activities during the last two years. They also received a lot of personal assistance. On the other hand, for most, there was a feeling of social deficiency that had the effect of rendering them lonely, disappointed in other people or unable to do everything in life that they wished.

Vulnerability

The mean and median age of the elder parent represented through the interviewed sample was 79.4 and 82 years respectively (range 69-89). Sixty percent were in their eighties. Eighty-seven percent lived with the abusing adult offspring at least some of the last two years. Only one lived alone, and one with her husband.

By and large, the elder parent suffered poor physical and emotional health (40.0% and 53.3% respectively). Physical health problems were usually chronic illnesses with disabilities (60.0%); emotional health problems were typically organic brain disorders (46.7%). Every elder parent had some physical health problems, although two lacked any emotional health problem. Represented physical health problems included poor eyesight, paralysis from a stroke, and emphysema resulting in breathing difficulties. Represented emotional health problems included depression, Alzheimer's disease, and schizophrenia.

When asked to describe the elder parent, the tone of most descriptions turned out to be negative (53.3%). Moreover, the topic of the subjects' description tended to be their relationship with the elder parent or the elder parent's relationship with other people (53.3%) rather than a description of the elder parent her or himself. For example, one respondent considered the elder parent "intelligent, but self-centered. [He's] only interested in himself and his friends. He never did anything for his family." Another described her mother as having "no interest in anything. She complains she can't see to read or watch television. She just wants to sit and find someone to call and complain."

In summary, the elder parent represented through the interviewed sample could be described as very old and chronically impaired, usually both physically and emotionally. She or he tended to live with the abusing adult offspring much of the last two years. However, the relationship between the two during that time had been such that the adult offspring viewed the elder parent unfavorably.

Abuse Socialization

Abuse socialization was explored in three ways. First, questions were asked on how the subjects were disciplined as children and how their parents behaved when angry with one another. Next, inquiry was made into the subjects' relations with other adult kin during their early years. Finally, the modified version of the Conflict Tactics Scale developed for this study was used to measure the type and frequency of violence and other tactics employed by the subjects and their parents in handling disagreements when the subjects were children.

When growing up, the interviewed sample was usually disciplined by being slapped or spanked (20.0%) or hit with something (33.3%). Some were not disciplined by their parents at all (20.0%). Only one subject was typically beaten. Combining this last response with those indicating that the usual discipline was being hit with something suggests that for the largest number of subjects (40.0%), severe violence was the discipline preferred by parents over reasoning, verbal or symbolic aggression, or less severe violence.

This pattern of responses contrasted with those obtained through use of the modified Conflict Tactics Scale. When asked to address the various means used by their parents to handle disputes with the subjects during childhood, rarely was the use of any form of severe violence acknowledged. Only slapping or spanking was regarded as a common tactic within the Violence Scale (used at least once or twice for 73.3% of the subjects). Just as typically, the methods for handling disputes were forms of reasoning or verbal or symbolic aggression. In fact, except for slapping or spanking and discussing the issue calmly (53.3%), none of the various tactics were employed by a majority of the parents of the interviewed sample. Only four subjects (26.7%) acknowledged being hit, and none or only one identified any other form of severe violence during childhood. Among the forms of less severe violence, excluding slapping or spanking, only four parents (26.7%) had pushed, grabbed, shoved or shook any subject and two (13.3%) had thrown something. Otherwise, less severe violence also was not a prevailing discipline mode by parents of subjects represented in the interviewed sample.

Overall, an average of only 1.7 forms of child abuse had occurred to the subjects during their childhood (potential range 0-13, actual range

0-7, *SD* 1.909). That average would drop to just 0.8 if slapping or spanking were eliminated from the list. This is probably justified, because for most Americans, slapping or spanking constitutes acceptable discipline of children and is done with neither the intent nor the effect of causing physical harm (Straus et al, 1980).

Indeed, content analysis of responses to open-ended questions as well as extraneous remarks for this section resulted in the discovery of only three subjects who indicated that they had observed or participated in family violence during childhood. One subject noted that he began physical abuse of the elder parent at age seven when he observed the elder parent hitting his wife. Violence became a relationship pattern between the two henceforth. This was also true of another subject, who said that as a child her mother hit her with "yardsticks, fly swatters, batons and switches," but that she dealt with conflict by pushing, slapping, kicking and hitting her mother. The remaining subject was a more passive recipient and spectator to family violence, as his psychotic mother came after his sister with a knife and beat him up. The father eventually sent him away to private boarding school for his safety.

Unlike the two subjects cited above who were violent to their parents during childhood, most subjects handled conflict with their parents by crying (60.0%) or discussing the issue calmly (53.3%). No form of violence was used.

Domestic violence also was not a pattern in the homes of the interviewed sample while growing up. In no home was the usual response of parents when angry with each other to use physical force or aggression. Most argued or yelled at the other spouse (53.3%). The second most typical response could be coded as discussing the issue calmly (20.0%). The majority of subjects as children were aware when their parents became angry and argued with one another. Sixty percent indicated that their parents usually argued in front of them. Just over a quarter of the subjects said that it happened when they were not around, and two were uncertain.

Almost all subjects had an adult relative with whom they had a particularly good relationship when growing up (86.7%). In most cases, this was an aunt or uncle. Only rarely was it the elder parent or other parent. The qualities which made these persons so special surrounded the relatives taking the subjects places (40.0%) or giving care (20.0%) or gifts (20.0%). As one respondent put it, "[Unlike the elder parent], they were there. They took care of me. They took me to lessons. They cleaned, cooked. They worried about me." Another appreciated his uncle taking him to baseball games, and still another because they hunted and fished together. Few subjects had an adult relative who was a problem growing up (20.0%). For those who did, the elder parent was most frequently mentioned.

In summary, slapping or spanking was the principal means by which the parents of the interviewed sample disciplined the subjects as children. When other means were employed, they tended to be either discussing the issue calmly or hitting with something. As children, the subjects responded to disagreements with their parents by crying or discussing the issue calmly. Domestic violence was rare among the parents. Expressed aggression took verbal or symbolic form. In addition, most subjects had adult relatives during childhood with whom they had particularly good relations. These relatives, usually aunts and uncles, brought joy and breaks in the routine for the subjects through care, gifts and excursions. Few subjects had a problem adult relative during childhood. For those who did, that relative was typically the elder parent.

Recent Abuse

The final part of the family conflict portion of the first interview concerned conflict tactics used during the last two years by the subjects and the elder parent. Once again the modified version of the Conflict Tactics Scale was used to measure this concept.

Responses suggested that for the adult offspring reasoning was the conflict tactic mode of choice, followed by verbal or symbolic aggression. Violence in any form, except pushing, grabbing, shoving or shaking, was rarely used. Only three subjects (20.0%) indicated the use of any form of severe violence.

The majority of subjects handled disagreements with the elder parent using one of three tactics, i.e., discussing the issue calmly (60.0%), getting information to back up an argument (53.3%) or stomping out of the room or house (60.0%). Less frequently they insulted or swore at the elder parent (46.7%), sulked or refused to talk about the issue (40.0%), cried (40.0%) or threw, smashed, hit or kicked something (40.0%). When violence was used, it most frequently took the form of pushing, grabbing, shoving or shaking the elder parent (46.7%). Although less common, throwing something at the elder parent (26.7%) and slapping or spanking the elder parent (26.7%) were still notable occurrences.

In completing the modified version of the Conflict Tactics Scale, 60.0 percent of all subjects acknowledged at least one act of violence against the elder parent during the last two years (average number of forms of violence per subject 1.6, range 0-7, *SD* 2.131). Among those who did, a range of between one and seven forms of violence were indicated (*M* 2.8). Some subjects also described the various violent acts in terms which expressed their own rationale for them. For example, one subject admitted that he could not handle his elder parent's dementia and resulting forgetfulness, which placed the household at considerable risk:

> The stove is really what did it. I came home and smelled gas. I opened the windows, and he started yelling at me, and he kept it up. I left and came back two days later and started beating him up. I nearly killed him.

Another considered his abuse as a defensive reaction "when my mother was hitting me on my arm and stomach and side."

It is interesting to note that 40.0 percent of the interviewed sample failed to acknowledge any violent act against the elder parent. This, of course, contradicts the information provided by the referral source caseworker which qualified the adult offspring for inclusion in the research sample. Looking more closely at the self-alleged nonabusers suggests some possible reasons for failure to admit elder abuse. In most instances, the reason probably rested with a fear of authority, and the perception that somehow I was an extension of that authority or at least in contact with it. Moreover, four of the six subjects comprising the group of self-alleged nonabusers could in general terms be described as submissive and dependent, mostly because of financial dependency on the elder parent, but also because their pathology, e.g., mental retardation or depression, usually made them docile. In the remaining two situations, the subject was either Appalachian, a culture noted for its reluctance to deal with outsiders (Weller, 1965; Riddell, 1974), or interviewed by the caseworker, and so perhaps fearful of bringing up the cause of the original report of the elder parent under Ohio's Protective Services Law for Adults. Notwithstanding, three of the six subjects in this group intimated the use of violence against the elder parent in other ways. More specifically, I twice observed one subject pushing, shoving or otherwise rough handling his father during the interviews conducted with him. For the other two subjects, intimidation was through extraneous remarks.

When conflict tactics were used by the elder parent in disputes with the adult offspring, they tended to take the form of verbal or symbolic aggression, such as doing or saying something spiteful (46.7%), insulting or swearing at the adult offspring (46.7%), sulking or refusing to talk about the issue (40.0%) or crying (40.0%). Occasionally some form of violence was used. Five respondents (33.3%) noted its used by the elder parent recently. In just one instance, however, did the violence take more than one form and occur more than once or twice. In that situation the elder parent was said to repeatedly slap, hit and beat up the adult offspring. This elder parent was the mother whose psychosis exhibited itself during the subject's childhood and who abused his sister and him at that time. The subject was very distressed by his mother's violence towards him. At various times he stated:

> My mother isn't sure at all that I live. I visited her on my birthday and she didn't remember it. In fact, that's when she hit me. . .[During the last two years] I'd no more than sit down and she'd beat me up. . .I am fearful of her using a knife [on me].

In summary, although most subjects admitted to abusing the elder parent during the last two years, a sizable number did not, perhaps out of a hesitancy to reveal such stigmatized behavior to an outsider and perceived authority figure. Reasoning was the conflict tactic mode of choice by adult offspring, verbal or symbolic aggression by the elder parent.

Second Interview

The second interview was an attempt to more fully explore three salient variables which had emerged during the first interview. These variables surrounded the dynamics of living or being in close contact with the elder parent, perceived lack of social support, and symptoms of pathology. Mostly open-ended questions were employed during the second interview to obtain information on these variables.

The presentation of findings for the second interview will follow the format used for the first. That is, results of the statistical analysis of responses to closed-ended questions will be followed by results based on the content analysis of responses to open-ended questions and extraneous remarks for each section of the interview. At the completion of findings from the second interview, there will be a presentation of results from still another content analysis. This one combined responses to open-ended questions and extraneous remarks from both interviews. It was done to provide integrative and further understanding to the etiology of elder abuse from repeated interviewing with the panel of adult offspring.

Living or Being with the Elder Parent

The interviewed sample averaged 11.2 years of living or having close contact with the elder parent during adulthood, including 19.6 months of the last two years. For most, living or being together recently was a positive experience (57.1%), usually because they liked the elder parent or they benefited directly from the arrangement (42.9%). For example, when asked why he liked being with his mother, one subject said, "She's my mom. I love her." Another replied, "It did better our relationship some. She helped me financially."

When living or being together was viewed negatively, the reason given was because of certain undesirable characteristics on the part of the elder parent or because the adult offspring felt stuck with the situation. In this regard, one subject described his mother as "very critical, fault-finding, hard to please." Another said that his elder parent "was not right in the head."

Most subjects felt that the elder parent had done things to make living or being together harder (64.3%). Often subjects were not specific around the nature of these behaviors (35.7%). When they were, the behaviors typically concerned the elder parent's refusal to do what was asked (42.9%).

Only a few subjects felt the elder parent had done things to make living or being together easier (35.7%), such as helping with finances or household tasks (21.4%) or offering sympathy or companionship (14.3%). Even those who felt the elder parent had tried to better the living situation usually either qualified their responses or expressed an overall unfavorable perspective on living with the elder parent. According to one subject, "There were occasional flashes of sympathy—a patting on the arm. Once in a while when we were going away for a few days, he would be okay for a day or so." To another subject, "He's company. Taking care of him is a chore."

The majority of subjects had thought about the elder parent living somewhere else (64.3%), ordinarily a nursing home (35.7%), with other relatives (14.3%) or on his or her own (14.3%). When alternative living arrangements had not been considered, it was usually beause other family members refused to take the elder parent, and this was the only desired alternative living arrangement.

Quite a few subjects had tried to get the elder parent to look into other living arrangements (42.6%). However, the arrangements were usually found to be unacceptable by the elder parent or adult offspring.

When placement of the elder parent was accomplished, it was only through order of the court or county department of human services (14.3%). Nonetheless, the subjects felt that if the elder parent became seriously ill or disabled, they would arrange for placement in a nursing home (78.6%), primarily because with that level of impairment the elder parent could not be handled at home (35.7%). In the few instances where nursing home placement would not be considered, it was because of cost, the unacceptability of nursing home care or preference to keep the elder parent at home.

Results of the Social Intimacy Index suggested that as a whole subjects had a balanced perspective around life with the elder parent (potential range 10-44, actual range 14-38, *M* 24.1, *SD* 8.781). On the positive side, living or being with the elder parent did not tend to make things feel crowded. Ninety-three percent of the subjects felt this way often or sometimes. Indeed, it was a comfort to have the elder parent around (64.3%), perhaps because the subjects and elder parent understood each other (71.4%) or the elder parent helped with household tasks to the extent she or he could (71.4%). On the negative side, subjects felt that most people would have a hard time living or being with the elder parent (85.7%). Certainly the elder parent's way of doing things drove the subjects' crazy (64.3%). Living or being with the elder parent also made for a lot of tension (71.4%).

Subjects were equally divided over whether or not they had the same problems with their elder parent now as they had in their household growing up, and whether or not the elder parent relied on them too much. Most subjects also felt that they cared for the elder parent in the same manner their parents cared for them as children (64.2%). The meaning of this last perspective varied by respondent. For some, this meant a replication of negligent care. After responding to the question, one subject added, "When my grandmother died, [the elder parent] just left me to fend for myself." For others, this meant duplicating loving care once received, e.g., "Emotionally in growing up, my mother was very giving to me."

Most subjects seldom or never felt that the elder parent did not do what was expected (57.1%). This was a surprising finding. Responses to questions during the first interview suggested that not doing what was expected was a quality of the elder parent that most subjects found disturbing, and a quality that most elder parents possessed. An explanation for these incongruous findings may rest with the wording of this question on the second interview schedule, i.e., "My elder parent doesn't do what's expected." Its negative phrasing may have been confusing to some respondents. This probability can be further gleaned from extraneous remarks made by some subjects which almost contradicted the score on the Likert-type scale that they gave for this item. For instance, one subject scored "never," but added, "She doesn't do nothing—only holler." Another who also scored "Never" said, "He always did the conventional thing, and this annoyed me."

Perhaps more than any other series question, those responses provided to the series of incomplete statements on the elder parent were most revealing of the depth of and rationale for the subjects' feelings regarding the elder parent. Overall, they suggested feelings negative in tone, feelings that existed because the elder parent would not do what was expected or was critical. In the opinion of the interviewed sample, the only way for things to get better would be if someone, especially the elder parent, was different. As things stood, the elder parent was not helpful or was most helpful when out of the way. Other people saw the elder parent more positively than did the subjects. For the latter, the elder parent was usually childlike and very different than the subjects in important respects.

More specifically, subjects felt living or being with the elder parent would be easier if the elder parent was different (42.6%), the subject was different (14.3%), or help was available (28.6%). Subjects would change the elder parent to make him or her less argumentive, less critical, more social or more cooperative.

For some subjects, the elder parent was always like a child (28.6%), for others never (14.3%). For most subjects, childishness was consistent with certain characteristics of the elder parent (50.0%), such as forgetfulness and indecisiveness.

The elder parent and subjects were more often seen as totally different from one another (28.6%) than not different at all (7.1%). When specific differences were acknowledged, subjects usually portrayed the elder parent as having the more conventional or more unacceptable characteristics, e.g., "She's real religious; I'm not" and "I am sane, and she is insane." Unlike the subjects themselves, other people were seen as finding the elder parent sweet or nice (35.7%) or incapable of managing (14.3%).

In describing when they became angry with the elder parent, the subjects also in part revealed when they became abusive. Although this will be explored in greater detail later in this chapter, suffice it to say at this time that the quality in the elder parent or subject that provoked or exacerbated anger was usually the same quality which provoked or exacerbated abuse. On the part of the elder parent, the quality was not doing what was expected (35.7%), being critical or negative (21.4%), interfering (14.3%), or acting violent (7.1%). On the part of the adult offspring, the quality was a generally angry state of mind (14.3%) or drunkenness (7.1%). One subject identified the quality in his father that most provoked his anger by saying, "He argues with me, talks back, gets contrary." Another described his father-in-law in this regard as a person who "doesn't cooperate and doesn't listen."

The depth of ill-feeling toward the elder parent was most revealed in the completion statements for "My elder parent helps me out by. . ." The largest number of responses could be coded "not at all or by staying out of the way" (35.7%). Related comments included "no way" and "keeping her mouth shut." Some subjects did, however, acknowledge specific help received from the elder parent, such as financial assistance (28.6%) or doing household chores (28.6%).

Despite these ill-feelings, nearly all adult offspring assumed the caregiving role for the elder parent out of duty (42.8%) or love or desire (21.4%). A minority assumed it because no one else would (35.7%). One subject called it "the righteous thing to do." Another said, "it was expected of me since childhood. I feel like I was programmed for this purpose."

Finally, the vast majority of subjects felt that the elder parent had changed in undesirable ways (85.7%). In most cases, the change rendered the elder parent less physically or mentally able. For instance, the elder parent was seen as "getting up there," "more forgetful" or "dependent." Other changes surrounded the personality of the elder parent (35.7%), with that individual seen as more "secretive," "prejudiced" or "exaggerated." Only two subjects described positive changes in the elder parent, and even these were qualified, i.e., "She *finally* let me do things for her" and "She's a *little* more emotionally stable." (Italics is used to suggest where emphasis was placed by the subject.)

By way of summary, the interviewed sample had spent considerable time in close proximity (usually residence) with the elder parent during adulthood, especially during the last two years. For most, this was a mixed blessing. They may have assumed caregiving responsibilities for the elder parent out of love or duty. The elder parent may have tried to make it work by helping financially or with specific tasks. And in some ways the situation had worked. Subjects were generally glad to be caring for the elder parent and felt comfortable in her or his presence. On the other hand, there were lots of problems with this living or caregiving arrangement. Much of the blame for these problems was seen to rest with the elder parent who did things to make living or being together harder, and who behaved one way with strangers but quite a different way with the subjects. Anyone would have difficulty living or being with the elder parent, it would seem alternative living arrangements, however, were usually unacceptable, unavailable or had failed. Therefore, faced with a situation that offered little escape, ill-feeling set the tone for interaction with the elder parent and anger became the by-product when expectations or personalities clashed.

Perception of Social Support

In describing the qualities important to friendship, family or neighbors, the subjects showed similarity across relationship types. However, there was variation in the emphasis placed on particular qualities between relationship types. More specifically, the most important quality for good neighbors was seen as the provision of instrumental support (42.9%), followed by similarity of experiences (21.4%). For family, it was emotional support (35.7%), followed by dependability (21.4%), with instrumental support less frequently mentioned (14.3%). For friendship, emotional and instrumental support were seen as equally important (28.6% each), and more so than longevity of the relationship (14.3%).

Two patterns of responses were especially noteworthy in this set of questions. First, nearly a quarter of the interviewed sample either lacked persons to use in illustration of the concept (i.e., they lacked friends, contact with family or good relations with neighbors), or the persons they did use were not seen to possess any positive qualities. This further suggests the social isolation found to characterize many subjects. Second, nearly one-third of the interviewed sample made reference to the elder parent in responding to these questions. For instance, the friend of one subject was special, because, "She's sympathetic to my plight with my mother. I don't know what else about her is good." Another appreciated a few neighbors who "knew the old man wasn't right." It might be that attitude toward the elder parent was used as a criterion for evaluating the subject's relationship with others. It might also be that since the subjects were being interviewed about the elder parent, this framed their responses to all questions, including these.

Among those who had a friend, family members or neighbor to use as reference, nearly one-third said these persons were missing something important in their relationship. Sometimes that quality explicitly related to the elder parent. For example, the friends of one subject were said to lack "common sense," because in situations with the elder parent, "They judged before they knew what was going on." Other times, the relationship with the elder parent was more implicit but present nonetheless, e.g., "I don't know her real well—she's only been here a year. She has problems of her own." The remaining subjects selected as missing qualities particular personality or other traits of their close associates, e.g., "She can be very detached at times" and "He can't speak much English."

Eleven subjects (78.6%) cited an instance when a friend, relative or neighbor lifted them up when the situation with the elder parent was getting them down. When the source of that support was identified (72.7%), it was usually a friend (50.0%). Relatives and others were mentioned less frequently (25.0% each). The type of support provided was almost equally divided between instrumental support (54.5%) and emotional support (45.5%).

In addition, seven subjects (50.0%) cited an instance when a friend, relative or neighbor let them down with respect to the elder parent. The source of disappointment nearly always was a relative (85.7%), the type of support expected but not received was equally emotional support and instrumental support.

When these findings are combined with those describing qualities important to friendship, family and good neighbors, the origins of perceived lack of social support on the part of many subjects (as indicated during the first interview) can be discerned. By and large, friends were seen to fulfill the expectations subjects had for them. Friends were the ones usually there to lend a hand or listen when there were problems with the elder parent, e.g., "My friends were support for me with regard to him" and "My friend took care of him for three days while I was out of town." In contrast, relatives were a disappointment and the likely source of many subjects' perceived lack of social support. They were usually expected to provide emotional support and be dependable, and more often than not they failed, e.g., "My relatives never took my side, but they never saw him at home" and "They said they were coming to visit or watch him, and they never showed up."

The relatives most commonly a disappointment were not those who comprised the subjects' household, if there were any besides the elder parent. Nearly every subject, for example, felt that their current marital status provided some measure of help in caring for the elder parent (92.9%). For married subjects, the spouse offered instrumental support, emotional support or both. For unmarried subjects, being single meant the freedom to devote oneself to caregiving as needed. Slightly over half of the subjects (57.1%) also identified something about their current marital status which made elder caregiving more difficult. For married subjects, this usually meant dividing one's attention between the elder parent and spouse. For unmarried subjects, it meant the lack of someone in the household on whom to depend for help.

The disappointing family members were primarily siblings and secondarily aunts and uncles. When responses or remarks from both interviews were considered collectively, they were most frequently mentioned as having been deficient in either caring for the elder parent or supporting the subjects in the caregiving role. To illustrate, one subject expressed disappointment in "my uncle, when he didn't send a nurse when both my mother and I were not well after saying she should have a nurse." Another complained, "My sister was supposed to take care of my mother and she didn't." Still another felt that his "brother and two sisters have detached themselves from any of her needs."

Individual Problems

To better understand the symptoms of emotional distress and pathology which characterized the interviewed sample, subjects were asked to indicate how often during the last two years they experienced specified symptoms largely derived from the Psychiatric Status Schedule. They were then asked if the origins of identified symptoms rested with interactions with the elder parent.

An average of 11.2 symptoms from the 29-item list were identified per subject as having been experienced often or sometimes during the last two years (range 4-17, *SD* 4.360). Those most frequently named as often being a problem were as follows: worried a lot (57.1%), stayed home a great deal (50.0%), had trouble sleeping (42.9%), felt angry a lot (42.9%) and felt anxious (42.9%). Eleven subjects (78.6%) attributed at least some of the identified symptoms to being around the elder parent. When asked which problems had this origin, the most common responses were "all of them" or "most of them" (45.5%). When respondents were specific, their listing generally included worried a lot, stayed home a great deal, felt angry a lot, felt anxious and felt sad a lot.

Content analysis of extraneous remarks made in relation to this portion of the interview revealed how greatly the subjects were burdened by symptoms and how much the symptoms were seen to originate with the elder parent. One subject described his appetite as improving with the death of his father, "[Before] I'd go off on beer diets." Another revealed, "My mother living here has made me and my husband more fearful of the future. He's very concerned about his becoming ill and depending on me." Still another subject was depressed about her mother, "and tired as a reaction to the depression."

Content Analysis of First and Second Interview Responses Combined

In order to elicit the full meaning of responses and remarks made by the interviewed sample from the two interviews, all recorded responses to open-ended questions and extraneous remarks from both interviews were collected, combined and content analyzed for themes. Themes were defined for the purposes of this study as characteristics exhibited by sizable numbers of subjects. A theme was considered primary if it characterized at least two-thirds of the subjects, secondary if it characterized at least one-third but less than two-thirds of the subjects. Five primary and nine secondary themes were identified.

The five primary themes were as follows: (1) The elder parent is seen as demanding, uncooperative or not doing what is expected. (2) The adult offspring is financially dependent on the elder parent, desires the resources of the elder parent, or is allegedly exploitive of the elder parent. (3) Individual pathology characterizes the adult offspring. (4) The adult offspring has relationship problems with neighbors or other family members. (5) The adult offspring is complaining and negative about the elder parent, but the reverse is also seen as true.

The nine secondary themes were as follows: (1) The adult offspring expects help and support from other family members around caring for the elder parent, but feels help and support are not extended. (2) A felt responsibility has kept the adult offspring hooked into the caregiver role for the elder parent. (3) The adult offspring feels that other people do not realize what it is like caring for the elder parent. (4) The adult offspring is the elder parent's only child, only living child or only capable child. (5) There have been long term relationship problems between the adult offspring and elder parent. (6) The adult offspring is not sympathetic to the elder parent's impairment status. (7) The elder parent is considered a "mental case" with resulting disturbing behavioral patterns. (8) The adult offspring shows a reluctance to seek help or advice. (9) The adult offspring prefers the elder parent passive, asleep or dead.

The overall profile of the abusing adult offspring that emerged from primary themes and those secondary themes which characterized nearly one-half of the interviewed sample suggested pathological individuals who either depended on or exploited the elder parent financially. They had relationship problems with the elder parent. They complained about the elder parent, seeing her or him as demanding, uncooperative or contrary. However, they also perceived the elder parent to complain about them in return. Nonetheless, they remained caregivers to the elder parent out of a sense of responsibility. In so doing, they felt quite alone in the experience. In part, this was because they had no sibling to whom to turn for help. In part, too, this resulted from expecting help and support from family and not having them extended. Other people simply did not realize what it was like taking care of the elder. In the final analysis, this made for relationship problems with family members and others as well.

Other characteristics were identified for smaller numbers of subjects within the interviewed sample. When they were combined with the primary and secondary themes, three distinct groups of subjects emerged. Each of these groups will be described by number of representative subjects as well as dominant themes and characteristics.

The Hostiles

I have labeled the first group "the hostiles." There were five subjects whose responses or remarks enabled their inclusion in this group. Unlike any of the other groups, the hostiles were noted for having long term relationship problems with the elder parent, considering the elder parent a "mental case," preferring the elder parent passive or dead, being hooked into caring for the elder parent through felt responsibility, having a history of intergenerational abuse, and feeling other family members expected the subject to be caregiver to the elder parent.

The hostiles were also distinctive in other ways. Members of the group were the only subjects that I had to be in the "right frame of mind" to interview a second time. They were challenging and pointed in their remarks, angry, suspicious and tense. Their overall anger and hostility for the elder parent and other persons was evident in words, facial expressions and general mannerisms. The field notes following interviews with these subjects were unique in the use of such descriptive terms as aggressive, macho, hates authority, outspoken and angry at everyone. Members of this group were articulate and talkative; as a whole, interviews with them lasted longer than with other subjects.

Looking also at closed-ended responses for the hostiles, group members were found to be the best educated of the three groups, but they saw themselves as underachievers. Often the elder parent was blamed for this. According to one subject, "My mother wouldn't let me go to Dyke College. No, I had to go to Miami and get a sociology degree. Now I couldn't work if I wanted to." In addition, the hostiles were the least likely to live all of the time with the elder parent during the last two years, the most likely to feel that the elder parent had done things to make being together harder, and the most likely to have experienced recent life crisis events. They provided less care or the same amount of care to the elder parent as other groups, but found it the most burdensome. Indeed, generally they found contact with the elder parent a very negative experience, and they were the most abusive as adult offspring. A composite casestudy for the hostiles follows:

> John always hated his mother. Their personalities were so different. Whereas she seemed dictatorial and conventional, he saw himself as sensitive and enlightened.
>
> John and his mother had fought since he was a child. Even then their conflicts were often quite brutal. There was the usual name-calling and threats. In addition, sometimes John's mother hit him with paddles and switches, plus twice with a bat, and he hit her with his fists and threw things.
>
> Actually, John and his mother spent little time together during his childhood. She always seemed to be busy, working at her job or attending various club meetings, where she invariably was the officer. John often wondered why she had decided to have a child. He had clearly been a bother to her.
>
> Throughout most of his adult years, John had little contact with his mother. He graduated from college and established himself in a profession. However, his success on the job was marred by conflicts with his superiors. He had been fired twice, once for hitting his supervisor. Home life also has been difficult. A stormy marriage ended in divorce after six years.
>
> John had a few friends. They were a support to him, listening to his troubles, most of which recently involved his mother. However, the neighbors and his relatives were a problem to John. They always seemed to criticize him. In their eyes, he never did anything right.
>
> During the past few years, John's mother had demanded more and more attention from him. It seemed unfair. She gave him virtually nothing during childhood, and now she wanted help in old age. It was not as if she was especially sick and impaired. Mostly she just tried to make people think she was. She was a "mental case," but also she had a way of making those around her one as well.
>
> John himself had spent quite a number of years in therapy, largely around problems with his mother. Not that it had helped all that much. He still felt angry everytime he was in her presence. He still wanted to hit her whenever she badgered him, which she constantly seemed to do.

Indeed, John's mother seldom left him at peace. She would call with her demands on evenings and weekends, sometimes even in the middle of the night. She seemed to consider him at her "beck and call," and everything was an "emergency."

John tried to avoid his mother, but he never could for long. She would not permit it. Moreover, he felt responsible for her care, largely because he was her only child and it was his role to be dutiful son, as he was frequently reminded by his aunts and uncles. That did not make him like her or wish her other than dead, however. She was a burden and irritation to John. She was also the source of his near constant anxiety and insomnia.

Perhaps the only benefit of their relationship for John was that his mother lent him money on occasion. Yet, even this had its drawbacks. John was forever berated by his mother for his poor investments and alleged frivolous use of money. The last time she did this, he punched her in the face and pushed her into the car. They had just left the bank, after her making a withdrawal for him.

The Authoritarians

I labeled the second group "the authoritarians." As a whole, they embodied the qualities of the authoritarian personality, a concept first defined by Adorno et al (1950) and later refined by others (e.g., for a review see Kirscht and Dillehay, 1967; Ray, 1981). The literature suggests that authoritarians are essentially rigid, punitive, ethnocentric, intolerant of ambiguity, domineering of subordinates and servile to superiors. Nonetheless, they are not mentally ill or pathological (Freedman et al, 1956).

This was true of the four subjects comprising this group of abusing adult offspring. They alone among the interviewed sample were not characterized by any kind of pathology. They, however, were rigid in their expectations regarding the elder parent, had a need for control, were inflexible with respect to household and other standards, and punished the elder parent for failure to comply with established norms. In the words of one member of this group, "I expect others to do what I would do. This makes me disappointed in people." The attitude was echoed by another subject who said, "I only get angry at things I can control, or other people can, and they don't — this upsets me."

The authoritarians also described their parents as having been authoritarian as well. For example,

When I was a kid, my parents said that as long as I was under their roof I had to do what was asked of me. Now, Mom is under my roof. . . There's no difference really [between my mom and me] — stubborn, bullheaded. We were raised with standards that had to be maintained.

Besides having authoritarian traits and authoritarian parents, this group was unique in several other ways. Members were not very sympathetic to the elder parent's impairment status. This may in part reflect their pragmatic attitude toward life. As one subject indicated, "If I have a problem, I try to solve it." He could not understand why his mother did not likewise make more of an effort to overcome the limitations imposed by her stroke.

Authoritarians also tended to infantilize the elder parent. According to one subject, her mother was "like a child for me. I always preferred preschoolers. I enjoyed brushing her hair and shopping for her. She was always so cute and petite." In addition, authoritarians treated the elder parent like they were treated as children, including inflicting on the elder parent the same level of abuse as had occurred to them as children.

When discussing the elder parent, the authoritarians usually began in a positive tone, but quickly moved to a more negative one. They were particularly resentful when the elder parent made "private matters" public and when they perceived the elder parent preferring others to the adult offspring. In the former regard, one embittered subject said, "She became very secretive. She didn't confide. She confided outside of the home. The result is that she is in a nursing home." In the latter regard, another subject stated, "My sister is my mother's baby. When she's here, my mama's always calling her." This angered the subject all the more, because she felt the sister was seldom around and provided little care for the elder parent.

Despite some of the ill-feeling attached to caregiving and the elder parent, authoritarians found other living or caregiving arrangements for the elder parent unacceptable. One subject concluded, "I wanted to take care of her, to keep her out of a nursing home."

Field notes from interviews with the authoritarians were laced with such adjectives as critical, impatient and bluntly honest. Furthermore, members of the group needed to justify actions that might suggest other than optimal treatment of the elder parent.

Considering responses to closed-ended questions, other traits emerged for the authoritarians. Generally speaking, they were the only married subjects (conventional behavior for adults and, therefore, to be expected of authoritarians). Although they had less education than the hostiles, they were just as likely to be working for pay or as a home-maker and earning in excess of $10,000 per year (again conforming with traditional American values). They were also more likely to have the elder parent living with them all or most of the last two years, and to like it. Finally, authoritarians provided the largest number of types of care to the elder parent, but found it less burdensome than did the hostiles. A composite casestudy of the authoritarians follows:

> Louise could not understand why her mother was not more grateful. For five years Louise had prepared the meals, done the laundry, arranged medical appointments, and performed a thousand other caregiving tasks.
>
> Louise had given her mother the attention that ordinarily would have gone to her husband and children. Not that Louise had minded. She like being home and taking care of someone who needed her. In some ways, it was like taking care of her children when they were infants. Her mother had to be dressed and changed, just as they had. The trouble was, her mother was not grateful for Louise's help.
>
> Louise found it quite a time-consuming responsibility to run a household. The house had to be kept clean, people's needs had to be met. Most of the time things went quite smoothly. Everyone did her or his part. All of that order broke down when Louise's mother had to have her own way. For example, she would not take baths, only showers, because her arthritis made getting in and out of the tub hard. Baths were better for soaking, however. She would not have breakfast with the family, wanting them to have some private time. This only made for two meal preparations, however.
>
> Louise tried to change her mother of these bad habits. At first she coaxed and then she threatened. When these failed, Louise used physical force. She pushed her mother into the tub. She shoved her down the stairs to breakfast. The actions were justified in Louise's estimation. Her mother had to learn to mind, just as she had expected Louise to mind when Louise was a child. It was unfortunate that her mother got hurt in the process, but she might learn faster that way.
>
> Another source of aggravation to Louise was her mother's seeming preference of her church friends to Louise. She looked for opportunities to be out of the house and with them. They also were the ones with whom she confided. Louise resented that she told them about the "push" in the tub and "shove" down the stairs. It was none of their business. Anyway, they had no idea what it was like caring for an elderly parent. If her mother persisted in these indiscretions, then Louise would be forced to have her live somewhere else, perhaps a nursing home. If that happened, it would be her mother's "choice," not Louise's.

The Dependents

The last of the three groups was labeled "the dependents." This group was less clearly defined by unique themes or characteristics than were the others. Indeed, what was perhaps most notable about the dependents in this regard was their lack of distinctive theme or characteristic.

Except for the fact that every member of the group was financially dependent on the elder parent and nearly all had lived the entirety of the last two years with the elder parent, no designated theme or characteristic was unique to this group. The cluster of traits identifying members of the group came more from field notes taken following interviews with the subjects than through content analysis of their responses or remarks. My overall feeling after being with the dependents was that they represented rather pathetic, immature adults. The dependents had never achieved the social, economic or emotional status expected of American adults. Rather, they seemed to remain attached to the elder parent in a child-like dependency, impassive in their desire to alter the present situation. Field notes following interviews with the dependents included such terms as unkempt appearance, neglected surroundings, quiet, brief responses, unanimated, socially uncomfortable and passive cooperation.

Looking at responses to closed-ended questions suggested that the dependents were unmarried, poorly educated, not working and low income. As a group they were ambivalent about what it had been like living with the elder parent during the last two years. Among the three groups, the dependents had the fewest formal contacts and participated in the fewest social and formal activities. They provided the least help to the elder parent, experienced the fewer stressor events, and were the least likely to admit to the infliction of elder abuse. Interviews with them also were the shortest. A composite casestudy of the dependents is found below:

> Except for two years in the Army, Martin had lived with his father all of his adult years. It was not as if they felt particularly close, however, it was only that living together met some of both of their needs. For Martin that meant a home and financial assistance. He had been unemployed for a long time. For his father that meant someone around to help when needed. He was blind.
>
> Martin spent much of each day at the neighborhood bar. He rarely spoke to anyone. He might shoot a few games of pool, but mostly he sat, and drank.
>
> Loneliness was characteristic of Martin. He had no friends, and his only neighbors were Puerto Rican, and so he didn't bother with them. Outside the bar, he spent his time at home. Actually Martin was never someone to go places and do things. That usually required other people, and even during childhood, they were lacking in Martin's life.
>
> Martin wished that his brothers were more help with their father. They left him to Martin, because Martin was single and they were not. Notwithstanding, they seldom telephoned, and even less often visited. At times Martin felt angry at their neglect.

Usually Martin and his father got along all right. However, once in a while they argued, especially when his father called Martin a drunk and pressured him to seek work. A couple times Martin even hit his father for that. Mostly he just left the house, slamming the door behind him.

Other

Only one subject of the interviewed sample could not be placed in any designated group. Throughout both interviews his responses and remarks were uniquely positive in tone regarding the elder parent and his life situation. He also was the subject whose pathology was mental retardation.

There is some evidence to suggest that adults who are mentally retarded but score high on self-maintenance scales also tend to score high in life satisfaction (Wood and Mueller, 1970) The subject in this study whose pathology was mental retardation was well able to maintain himself in both home and sheltered work settings. He took care of the household along with his mother and pets. This included doing the laundry, cleaning house and running errands. In addition, the subject left the house every weekday for sheltered work on the other side of town, for which he used public transportation.

My impression after twice interviewing the subject was that generally his life aspirations matched his life experiences, and as a result, he was satisfied. The only exceptions were clearly noted by him during interview. That is, he was displeased when a boy threw a snowball at him, his mother awakened him by dropping something on the floor, and his former fiance left to return to her ex-husband.

Special Appalachian Interview

Interviews were conducted with two purposively selected natives of Appalachia to determine the acceptance of physical force in handling disputes between adults and the prevalence of family violence in that culture. The need for these interviews arose when one subject among the interviewed sample expressed an easy acceptance of such acts as slapping or spanking her mother that was not exhibited by other subjects. It was suspected that her Appalachian background may have contributed to this attitude. Certainly, the literature on Appalachian culture suggests that physical force is used within families to control and subordinate certain members, usually wives and children (Kunkin and Byrne, 1972; Hennan and Photiades, 1979).

Both Appalachian subjects were middle-aged or elderly, born in West Virginia and spent at least their first eighteen years there. The parents of both were born and raised in either West Virginia or Kentucky; the fathers worked as coal miners, carpenters or factory laborers.

Both subjects described the use of firm child discipline techniques by, and domestic violence between, their parents. According to one subject, "My mother laid it on me with a switch. She had an awful temper. She would beat me so bad that my lips would swell back, and I'd be all bloody." The other said that when her parents were angry, "They would hit each other. There were lots of black eyes and stitches. It was both of them doing it about every weekend." Arguing occurred in front of the children.

Both Appalachian subjects also readily described incidents of violence between older adults that they had observed in growing up. Using the nine-item modified Violence Scale of the Conflict Tactics Scale, each of them had observed seven or eight identified forms of violence. Neither had observed someone burn or try to burn another, and one had not seen anyone use or threaten to use a knife or gun. Otherwise, all identified acts of violence had been observed, and usually quite often. As one respondent described it,

> All my family on my mother's side would have drinking parties and fight and knock each other down and throw things. The fights would usually happen over little things. It was the alcohol that did it. They couldn't handle drink.

Only one of the two Appalachian subjects acknowledged causing physical pain or injury to any person growing up. She admitted to "beating up" her brother, "whipping" her cousin, and smashing a lunch box over the head of a classmate who "spit in my face." The other subject said that she was too timid as a child to inflict harm.

Both subjects claimed that their childhood friends had been "pretty rough. They'd get into fights. They'd pull hair, scratch." It was seen as a way of life, something that everyone did. This perspective on violence was reflected in the subjects' reaction to its occurrence, which was to ignore it.

Responses to incomplete sentences suggested that in Appalachian culture old people were treated with respect, men considered themselves dominant, family stuck together and supported one another against attacks by outsiders, and hitting was acceptable with outsiders and when the other person "deserved it."

When asked specifically about elder abuse in Appalachia, the subjects stated that although it was not acceptable for a child to hit an elder, it was acceptable for an adult to do so. One subject gave two examples of elder abuse broadly defined among her associates in West Virginia. In one instance, a young man hit an elder for breaking something in a store. In the other, the respondent's sister operated a board and care home and systematically exploited residents to gain their resources.

Maltreatment remains part of the lifestyle of one subject, although she has spent over thirty years outside of Appalachia. She admitted striking her husband, "He accused me of going out with this colored man. So I took these rocks in both hands and hit him across the head." At the time of the interview, she was planning to leave her daughter's home, because "all she does is pick and fight and take my money."

In conclusion, the interviews with representatives of Appalachian culture revealed an easy acceptance of violence and family abuse, including elder abuse. They serve to explain the ability of the Appalachian subject among the interviewed sample to describe potential or actual abuse of her mother as normative behavior.

Discussion

Reconsidering the Conceptual Framework

The purpose of this study was to explain the etiology of elder abuse by filial caregivers. This was done by testing a conceptual framework which uniquely integrated suggested etiologies for abuse occurrence from the elder abuse literature. The specific constructs which comprised the conceptual framework determined the topics of initial inquiry during interview with a panel of abusing adult offspring. Second interview with the panel explored variables for explaining elder abuse found salient during initial interview.

Based on research findings, there was a need to revise the study's conceptual framework for explaining elder abuse. The original suggested that elder abuse by filial caregivers resulted when the caregivers had been socialized to regard abuse as a possible expression of frustration and elders as less than human. In addition, the presence of one or more of three possible conditions was required. First, chronic structural or contextual factors increased the stress level of the caregivers. Second, the caregivers possessed pathological characteristics which increased their tolerance for abuse or decreased their tolerance for stress. Third, conditions or characteristics increased the elder's vulnerability to abuse or inability to retaliate against it. Under these circumstances, elder abuse occured with acute stress as perceived by the caregivers.

There were some variables in the original conceptual framework which the elder abuse literature had suggested as being related to abuse occurrence for which the present study found no validating evidence, and other variables which had not been emphasized in the literature for which this study found evidence of their influence in abuse occurrence. As a consequence, one major and several minor revisions were made to the conceptual framework. The major revision was the elimination of chronic stress as an explanation for abuse occurrence. The minor revisions were as follows: (1) use of abuse socialization within the context of history of family violence or subcultural violence as a partial explanation for some but not all abuse situations, (2) inclusion of certain personality characteristics with pathological characteristics of the caregiver as increasing abuse or decreasing stress tolerance, (3) focus on characteristics rather than conditions of elders as increasing their vulnerability to abuse or inability to retaliate against it, (4) addition of perceived lack of social support by caregivers as a factor stimulating the effect of pathology and certain personality characteristics for increasing abuse or decreasing stress tolerance, and (5) addition of prolonged and profound intimacy between the elder and caregiver as stimulating the effect of all prior factors but especially elder vulnerability in facilitating abuse occurrence. Furthermore, rather than several potential pathways toward elder abuse by caregivers, the revised conceptual framework suggested only one.

Essentially, the revised conceptual framework postulated that for elder abuse to occur by filial caregivers, abuse must be regarded as normative behavior and ageism as prevailing attitude in the general culture. Abuse socialization was accelerated in addition when the caregivers' family of orientation was abusive or violence characterized the subculture in which they were raised. Having been socialized to abuse, however, elder abuse only actually occurred when four other conditions were met. First, the caregivers had pathological or personality characteristics which increased their tolerance for abuse infliction or decreased their tolerance of stress. The pathological characteristics included mental illness, mental retardation, emotional distress or alcohol abuse. The personality characteristics included authoritarianism or an abusive self-concept. Second, the caregivers perceived themselves without sufficient social support to perform the elder caregiver role. The particular source of desired but deficient social support was usually the caregivers' family. Third, the elder parent had characteristics that increased their vulnerability to abuse or inability to retaliate against it. Most importantly, these characteristics included physical or mental impairment. Fourth, the elder parent and caregiver were in close proximity and intimacy with each other for an extended time period. The usual basis for this was coresidence. Under these conditions, elder abuse by filial caregivers occurred when triggered by some situation of acute stress as perceived by the caregivers.

The revised conceptual framework described the conditions facilitating abuse occurrence for the subjects of the interviewed sample. Although there was variation among the subjects, it was variation of detail rather than overall etiology. The next several paragraphs in this chapter explain the revised conceptual framework and justify the various constructs comprising it based on summary findings from interviews with the interviewed sample.

Explaining the Revised Conceptual Framework

Chronic stress was eliminated from the revised conceptual framework. The interviewed sample did not seem to be characterized by external stress during the last two years. As a whole, they experienced few stressor events. In addition, they did not reside in crowded living situations. Although some had low incomes or lacked employment, these were not recent occurrences that required life adjustment. Rather, they had become situations characteristic of the subjects and to which most had made accommodations.

With regard to stress internal to the caregiving relationship, most subjects provided considerable care to the elder parent and did not find it bothersome. Instead of caregiving itself being a burden, subjects found specific behaviors on the part of the elder parent both unacceptable and frustrating. Most subjects were glad to assume the caregiving role, doing so out of sense of duty or love.

Abuse as normative behavior and ageism as a prevailing attitude in the American culture were not explored in this study. They were, however, assumed. On the other hand, inquiry was made into history of family violence and the influence of Appalachian cultural heritage for abuse socialization. The result of those investigations suggested that level of child abuse matched level of elder abuse. For example, those subjects who had suffered the most abuse by their parents as children were the most violent toward the elder parent in recent years. Furthermore, the acceptance of violence among family members, between adults and against elders in Appalachian culture explained the easy acceptance of elder abuse by the one subject of Appalachian heritage in this study.

Every subject of the interviewed sample was characterized by pathology or authoritarian personality. Specific reasons or remarks by the subjects also indicated that these characteristics influenced the subjects' ability to accept or handle the elder parent's behavior. Behavior on the part of the elder parent was more likely to be seen as demanding or uncooperative and so more likely to provoke anger or frustration by adult offspring, because the adult offspring was drunk, emotionally ill or distressed, intellectually deficient or characterized by rigid, abusive or other such personality traits.

Generally, the interviewed sample saw themselves alone in the caregiving role for the elder parent. Although many received help for specific tasks and support from friends and household members, they felt neglected by their extended family in terms of emotional and instrumental support. Sometimes this perception reflected a lack of available siblings to share the caregiving role. Other times it reflected the subjects' belief that their siblings or those of the elder parent was negligent. As a result, the interviewed sample felt trapped as caregivers. Unable to find refuge among kin and unable to give up caregiving responsibilities out of felt duty or love, the subjects were left to interact with the elder parent and provide care to the best of their abilities. Unfortunately, their pathology, personality characteristics, unresolved family conflict and other related factors left them ill-equipped to do so except at considerable cost.

Every elder parent represented through the interviewed sample was characterized by physical impairment, and nearly all by emotional or mental impairment as well. In addition, the elder parent tended to be of advanced old age. These characteristics meant that the elder parent depended on other persons to meet basic daily needs. With few, if any, other caregiving options available or acceptable than those offered by the abusing adult offspring, this had the effect of rendering the elder parent dependent on the adult offspring for care. Usually this dependency for care was coupled with the adult offsprings' dependency on or desire for the elder parent's financial resources. Under some circumstances, this may have resulted in a perception of balanced exchange between the elder parent and adult offspring. This was not so, however, when there prevailed conditions of abuse socialization, pathology or perceived lack of social support for the adult offspring, as happened with the interviewed sample. The pathology and other personality characteristics distorted the basis for achieving a perception of equitable exchange. The other factors further increased the costs seen to be associated with caregiving or interacting with the elder parent. Under these conditions, equity could never be achieved, and the adult offspring would always be in the more powerful position. One subject described the situation with her mother quite well when she said, "We had our battles when I was a kid, too. Now the power structure has changed, and I'm in power."

The final factor that established the conditions for elder abuse occurrence was prolonged and profound intimacy between the elder parent and adult offspring. Thirteen of the 15 subjects in the interviewed sample resided with the elder parent at the time of abuse infliction and had done so for many months, sometimes many years. The remaining subjects had spent considerable time with the elder parent in some kind of caregiving capacity. The old adage "familiarity breeds contempt" had special meaing for the subjects of this study. Day-in and day-out proximity with the elder parent reactivated old negative feelings and created new ones as well. Moreover, proximity now was different than when the subjects were children. Now the subjects were more able and held the greater power. Now, too, the elder parent was impaired and dependent for care. The elder parent often did not accept this impairment and dependent status and fought the consequences of both with the adult offspring. Furthermore, personality traits on the part of the elder parent perhaps barely acceptable to the subjects as children were totally unacceptable after years of adult status.

These then provided the conditions for abuse occurrence by the interviewed sample. When abuse actually happened, it was under circumstances of acute stress. Content analysis of responses to open-ended questions as well as extraneous remarks from both interviews enabled me to establish the sequence of events preceding actual abuse occurrence. This sequence identifies the dimensions of the acute stress construct and further refines the revised conceptual framework for this study.

The acute stress sequence had two phases. I labeled the first phase "the struggle." It had five steps. In step one, the adult offspring expected the elder parent to behave in a certain way, e.g., to take a bath or not criticize the adult offspring's spending habits. In step two, the elder parent did not behave as expected, e.g., refused to go upstairs for the bath or criticized the adult offspring. As a result, in steps three and four, the adult offspring perceived this contrary behavior as willful on the part of the elder parent and made further demands for the elder parent to comply. However, in step five, the elder parent refused to comply or did not even seem to listen to the adult offspring. This ended phase one of the acute stress sequence.

Phase two was labeled "the fight." It had four steps. In step one, the adult offspring got angry. Varying amounts of arguing occurred in step two. In step three, the adult offspring lost control, and in step four, became abusive.

To illustrate this sequence of events leading to abuse occurrence, I compiled the related comments of several subjects into a collective amount of elder abuse.

> He'd sneak up and look into my private things. There was nothing private from him. . .[He] can be a bit of a meddler. . .[He] didn't do what needs to be done. [He's] stubborn. . .At first I try to explain. . .[He] won't accept my advice. . .He doesn't cooperate and doesn't listen. . .It's difficult. . .I get mad. We argue. . .This upsets me. I become brutally frank. . .He argues with me, talks back, gets contrary. . .I threaten to kick his ass in. . .It all builds up until you don't know what's happening. . .At some point it gets out of control. . .I took [him] by the shoulders and shook [him]. Then you want to kill yourself for losing control.

Authoritarian personality and pathology have the effect of exasperating the acute stress sequence. For example, in phase one the adult offspring with an authoritarian personality may have more rigid expectations of how the elder parent should behave and greater conviction in the elder parent's ability to meet these expectations. Pathology, on the other hand, may distort reality and render the adult offspring so afflicted less able to accurately evaluate the need for or ability of the elder parent to behave in a particular manner. In phase two, the adult offspring with an authoritarian personality may believe that actions, even abusive actions, are justified as long as their intent is to modify undesirable behavior. In contrast, pathology may severely inhibit the afflicted adult offsprings' abilities at self-control or decrease their capabilities for understanding the effect of actions taken.

To exemplify the acute stress sequence for the adult offspring with an authoritarian personality, consider the following composite comments of one subject:

> She does not do what needs to be done—like putting on clean clothes, taking a bath. She's stubborn. She knows I can't make her. . .[I thrown something] when she's being disagreeable. . .Maybe in the shower [I pushed or shoved her].

As an instance of the effect of pathology on the acute stress sequence, consider the remarks of a subject afflicted by emotional distress, with a history of alcohol abuse:

> My mother started crying uncontrollably the other day. She couldn't get all the food I bought in the refrigerator. She said that we don't need all this food. I could hit her when she says, which she always does, "You have no common sense and judgment." I am afraid sometimes I am going to lose control and really hurt her. . .This is where the violence comes in—the criticalness. I am forced into trying to defend my position.

Correspondence Between Findings from Interviews with the Adult Offspring and Interviews with Their Caseworkers

It was important to determine the correspondence between responses given by the referral source caseworkers and those given by the interviewed sample for similar questions. This would suggest agreement between data sources and establish construct validity for findings.

There were eight response categories for which comparison could be made, i.e., age, marital status, employment status and annual income for the adult offspring; age and living arrangements for the elder parent; type of abuse for the most recent incident; and number of abuse incidents. This resulted in a total of 120 response comparisons (15 subjects multipled by 8 response categories). Comparisons of the two sources for the response categories resulted in the identification of 29 responses (24.2%) which failed to correspond.

In assessing these findings, it was concluded that a certain amount of failure to correspond could be explained by change in circumstances for the interviewed sample between the time of data collection from the referral source caseworkers to the time of data collection from the interviewed sample. For example, one subject who had previously been unemployed had secured work as a truck driver by the time of the first interview. This change in circumstance affected the responses for both employment status and annual income for the adult offspring.

An additional amount of failure to correspond represented approximation although not exact correspondence in responses. For instance, two subjects were described by their referral source caseworkers as being in their early fifties. When interviewed, the subjects claimed to be in their late forties. However, certain characteristics, e.g., disability and balding hair, made them appear older than their stated years.

Taking both of the above factors into consideration resulted in the identification of only 16 responses (13.3%) which still failed to correspond. In interpreting these, it would seem that a certain amount of failure to correspond resulted from a lack of knowledge on the part of the referral source caseworkers, i.e., age of the elder parent. A certain amount also probably resulted from stereotyping of the subjects by their caseworkers, i.e., annual income of the adult offspring. The remaining amount probably resulted from the inability of the interviewed sample to completely reveal behaviors that might be stigmatized or subject to sanction, i.e., type of abuse or number of abuse incidents. On the whole, however, there was substantial agreement between the two sets of responses. Where there was disagreement, it tended to occur in the response categories describing the elder abuse, as might be expected.

Comparison of Interview Findings with Other Sources

The findings from this study lend support to those from Wolf et al's (1984) research on elderly victims of physical abuse. Both investigations discovered pathology and financial or other dependency among the abusers. Both failed to substantiate history of family violence or external stress as etiologies for abuse occurrence. Moreover, both investigations found social isolation to characterize their subjects of study.

Wolf et al (1984) were the only other elder abuse researchers to focus exclusively on physical abuse and the etiology of abuse occurrence. The others were concerned with multiple forms of elder abuse and equally or more interested in the nature of the problem. As a result, there is greater comparability of findings between Wolf et al and this study and greater meaning in the uncovered similarity of results.

There were, however, differences in findings between the present study and Wolf et al's (1984) that should be mentioned. First, Wolf et al did not explore stress internal to the caregiving relationship. Indeed, it could not have been adequately done using a sample of abuse victims. Therefore, Wolf et al never discussed the effect of disturbing behaviors on the part of the elder parent and other such factors on abuse occurrence. The results of the present study did not indicate the importance of caregiver stress in explaining elder abuse. They did, however, suggest that factors associated with caregiving were important, particularly disturbing behaviors by the elder parent which made caregiving difficult or frustrating and lack of support from family for caregiving efforts which made the role of caregiver an isolating experience.

Second, Wolf et al's (1984) abused elders were not found to be more ill, impaired or functionally dependent than their control group. Most of the adult offspring in the present study perceived the elder parent to be in fair or poor health, and both physically and mentally impaired. It may be that the two studies do not so much differ as present alternative perspectives in this regard. Wolf et al presents the viewpoint of the elder parent. This study presents that of the adult offspring. The general impairment status of the elders in both instances may be the same, if judged by health professionals. However, impairment status can be seen very differently by the parties most affected. For an adult offspring ill-equipped to assume caregiving by virture of pathology and other factors already discussed, the impairments of the elder parent may seem severe and incapacitating. On this basis, impairment and dependency have meaning in explaining elder abuse but only in a context which considers the characteristics of the abuser that increase the impact of impairment or dependency on caregiving. Alone they have little meaning.

Another comparison needs to be made. This one considers the dynamics for elder abuse suggested by referral source caseworkers for this study and the results from repeated interviews with the interviewed sample. In this comparison, the referral source caseworkers found pathology for the abuser and impairment for the elder parent the leading contributors to abuse occurrence. They placed much less emphasis on stress or history of family violence. Mention, however, was made of Appalachian background as contributing to the abusive behavior of one adult offspring. In addition, such disturbing behaviors of the elder parent as aggression and lack of cooperation were occasionally indicated as influencing abuse occurrence. These findings correspond with those derived through interviews with the interviewed sample. They reinforce the saliency of the constructs comprising the revised conceptual framework of this study.

Agreement with both sources of data on elder abuse helps validate the findings of this study derived from repeated interview with abuse perpetrators. They suggest that the perceptions on abuse etiology are stable across research setting, design and subjects.

CHAPTER V

IMPLICATIONS AND CONCLUSIONS

OVERVIEW

ELDER ABUSE is the most recently recognized aspect of family violence. It is also a major social problem affecting the growing number of older Americans. Although research on the topic began in the late 1970s, its initial focus was largely limited to the nature and scope of the problem. Only beginning in the 1980s was serious inquiry made into the etiology of elder abuse. The findings from these studies show much variability. Part of the reason rests with the use of different operational definitions of elder abuse and other key concepts. Part, too, is due to the failure of any study to have as research subjects the abuse perpetrators themselves. As a result, research conclusions are based on second- or third-hand perceptions.

The present study explored the etiology of elder abuse by filial caregivers through in-depth, focused interviews with adult offspring known to have physically abused an elder parent. Questions during the first interview concerned explanations for elder abuse suggested in the literature which had been integrated into a proposed conceptual framework. Questions during the second interview explored in greater detail those variables in the framework found most salient for explaining abuse occurrence following initial questioning. Interviews were conducted with a total of 15 adult offspring identified by hospitals and human service agencies in Northeast Ohio. The referral sources identified another 25 qualifying offspring who were not interviewed, because they were unavailable, inappropriate or unwilling to be interviewed. Nonetheless, background information was obtained from referral source caseworkers on all 40 research subjects and was used to indicate the representativeness of the interviewed sample and to verify some of the findings obtained through interview with the interviewed sample. In addition, interviews were conducted with purposively selected representatives of the Appalachian culture to determine their attitude toward violence and elder abuse when it was found that one interviewed subject expressed an acceptance of elder abuse which was not apparent among others in the interviewed sample, and it was suspected that her Appalachian background was the origin of this attitude.

The results of this exploratory research suggested that the etiology of physical abuse of elderly parents by filial caregivers could be found in a conceptual framework which integrated abuse socialization, pathology or certain personality characteristics, social isolation and acute stress for the adult offspring; vulnerability for the elder parent; and intimacy between the adult offspring and elder parent.

The conceptual framework indicated that for elder abuse to occur the perpetrators had to be socialized to be abusive through learning pro-abuse norms, in some instances intensified through a history of family or subcultural violence. Moreover, they had to have pathological or authoritarian personality characteristics which increased their tolerance for abuse infliction or decreased their tolerance for stress. Under these conditions, they lacked the capacity to cope with the difficulties of providing care to a physically or mentally impaired elder parent. At times they were unable to understand or accept the behaviors or vulnerability of the elder parent. At times, too, they could find no release, other than abuse, from the frustrations and anger which arose after prolonged and profound contact with her or him. These filial caregivers believed that they were alone in caring for the elder parent. Committed to caring for the elder parent by felt responsibility or love, isolated in the caregiving role through perceived lack of family support, these adult offspring were primed for abuse inflictions, which occurred under circumstances of acute stress that followed a predictable pattern, beginning with perceived lack of compliance by the elder parent and ending with loss of control and abuse infliction by the adult offspring.

The results of this study offered a profile of the abusing adult offspring as a white, middle-aged man who is unmarried with some high school education. He is Catholic, works as an operator or laborer and earns between $15,000 and $20,000 annually. The elder parent that he abuses is his natural mother with whom he currently lives and has lived for several years. She is very old and both physically and mentally impaired.

The abusing adult offspring typically has inflicted three different forms of violence on his elder parent during recent years. Usually these forms include pushing, grabbing, shoving or shaking as well as throwing something at the elder parent and slapping or spanking her. Violence, however, is not the most common means by which the adult offspring handles conflict with the elder parent. Reasoning is more common, and verbal or symbolic aggression is the conflict tactic of choice by the elder parent.

The typical abusing adult offspring has some characteristic pathology, usually emotional distress, mental illness or alcoholism. He has not been stressed by recent life crisis events. He has, however, been burdened by close contact with the elder parent, particularly by her disturbing behaviors and his lack of available time for personal pursuits because of caregiving responsibilities. What makes the situation more unbearable for him is a perceived lack of support from family members, especially siblings or aunts and uncles. Either these relatives do not exist or they are unwilling to help. On this basis, the adult offspring is left to provide care to the elder parent in seeming isolation. Actually, although he often does provide considerable care, he does so with the assistance of others, usually household members or friends, and within a network of formal and informal contact and support.

Finally, the study's findings portrayed the abusing adult offspring as having grown up in a nonabusive home. Although he was slapped or spanked as a child, this is considered acceptable discipline in American society. Moreover, his parents usually handled disagreements with each other by arguing and yelling. They were rarely violent. The adult offspring also had aunts and uncles with whom he maintained particularly positive relations while growing up.

The revised conceptual framework for explaining elder abuse by filial caregivers and the profile of the abuser which emerged from this study represent advances in understanding elder abuse as a social problem. For the first time a conceptual framework for elder abuse was proposed and explored through empirical research that focused on a single form of abuse. For the first time the perpetrators were the focus of investigation. For the first time the etiology of elder abuse was examined through sequential interviews with research subjects.

The consequences of this study have been a verification of certain explanations of elder abuse previously suggested in the literature (i.e., pathology, social isolation and vulnerability); a questioning of other explanations (i.e., external stress and history of family violence, except under certain circumstances); an identification of new explanations (i.e., intimacy and acute stress); and an integration of salient explanations into a conceptual framework which provides understanding of the conditions and sequence of events leading to abuse occurrence. Furthermore, the meaning for an abusing adult offspring of being around and providing care to an elder parent has been clarified.

POLICY AND PROGRAM IMPLICATIONS

The present study offers risk indicators for elder abuse, including a profile of the abuser and description of events leading to abuse occurrence. This information is important to service providers and prospective filial caregivers alike. For service providers, it suggests means for detecting potentially abusive situations, and therefore the possibility of preventing abuse occurrence. For prospective caregivers, it provides a way of assessing the probability for abuse infliction. Prospective caregivers with a predominance of identified "abused-prone" characteristics may wish to seek alternatives to assuming the caregiving role for the elder parent.

The study indicates that the effect of assuming caregiving responsibilities when an adult offspring is ill-equipped to do so may be dangerous for the elder parent and emotionally damaging for the adult offspring. Social service agencies need to assist prospective caregivers in making this assessment and support them through counseling in caregiving decisions that are made. Since many of the abusing adult offspring in this study were employed and had no contact with social workers other than the adult protective service workers investigating the report of elder abuse, some of this assessment and counseling may need to originate in places of employment, perhaps as components of employee assistance programs, or through those other professionals, like physicians or clergy, with whom there is contact.

Current public policy emphasizes the importance of family, especially adult sons and daughters, in assuming greater responsibility for the care of elderly pesons. The rationale for this is both philosophically and fiscally based. Findings from this study suggest that not all adult offspring have the capability for assuming such responsibility. One interviewed subject offered his own advice for potential filial caregivers who lack the capabilities for the task when he ended the interview and said, "If you tell people something after this study, tell them, 'Don't do it, but walk away and find someone who can help, and don't listen to the others.' "

The costs of caregiving that results in abuse infliction are very great. They include expenditures for health care of abused elders and therapy for distraught adult offspring. They also include the physical and emotional damage to both parties which may be permanent and cannot be measured in dollars and cents. In this regard, it should be recalled that among the interviewed sample one adult offspring had recently attempted suicide and another had committed suicide over relations with the elder parent.

Public policy needs to support families that can effectively assume the caregiving role. However, it also needs to support families that decline this role in part by providing viable caregiving alternatives. Minimally, these altneratives should include the availability of sound, low cost and well-publicized residential facilities ranging from adult family care and assisted living through nursing home care. Housing alternatives such as these may decrease the need for coresidence of abusing adult offspring and elder parent, and so decrease the intimacy which can foster abuse occurrence.

The findings from this study have other policy and programming implications for health and human services. First, they suggest a need for hospitals and other health facilities to establish elder abuse detection centers or protocols. Although there were three hospitals among the potential referral sources for the study, only two situations of abuse were identified through this kind of setting. All three hospitals had established centers or protocols for child abuse detection. However, at the onset of the study, only one had done similarly for elder abuse. This is especially discouraging when it is realized that each hospital had on staff persons in administrative authority with knowledge or experience in the areas of elder abuse or adult protective services. For whatever reason, elder abuse detection centers or protocols were not established. As a result, it is likely that many instances of elder abuse have gone and continue to go undetected, and resulting pain or injuries are attributed to the aging process, effect of chronic illnesses or household accidents.

Second, findings from the present study suggest that mental health, mental retardation and alcoholism service systems need to become more involved in preventing and treating elder abuse. Since a major factor explaining physical abuse is pathology on the part of the perpetrator, the various service systems most concerned with pathology must assume roles in helping adult offspring so afflicted make appropriate decisions in caring for an elder parent. They also must provide the treatment needed to affect the emotional damage caused by caregiving inappropriately assumed. To date, few such service systems have become interested in elder abuse, and few prevention or treatment models have emerged from such systems.

In communities like Cleveland, which have formed consortiums or networks around elder abuse, it is common to have mental health boards and centers along with alcoholism councils as members. The next step should be their greater involvement in service planning and provision. Examples of programs that might be developed include support groups for adult offspring with "difficult" elder parents or who refuse to assume caregiving responsibilities but are burdened by guilt from making that decision.

It is important that the language used to describe these programs not suggest wrongdoing by the adult offspring. Otherwise, these persons are unlikely to become involved. Elder abuse is more tabooed than either child abuse or spouse abuse. Although historically there have been American social norms for the physical discipline of children and wives, no such norms have existed for the physical discipline of elder parents. It is perhaps for this reason that, as implied from this study, only "certain" adult sons and daughters are capable of elder abuse and then only under "certain" circumstances.

Third, the results of this study indicate that a variety of support services are required to prevent elder abuse by filial caregivers. Since most adult offspring in the study lacked available or willing family to assist with caregiving, for those who do assume the task, support must come from formal networks. The importance of this support cannot be overstated. One interviewed subject, particularly aware of her lack of family support and its effect on caring for her very impaired mother, said, "I think it's a hell of a thing to be an only child. I am a great advocate of big families."

Substitutes must be developed for deficient or delinquent family support. Substitutes should include respite care and homemaker-home health aide services. Although present in most communities, these services are usually too costly or difficult to arrange for many of the adult offspring with the characteristics identified through this research. In addition, financial support and employment counseling should be available to some filial caregivers, such as the "dependents" among the interviewed sample, to decrease their economic dependency and their need for coresidence with the elder parent.

To date, most of the policies and programs developed to prevent and treat elder abuse have been modeled after those used in child abuse. For example, most adult protective service laws are similar to child protective service laws. The findings from this study suggest that the etiology of elder abuse may be different from that of child abuse in some important respects. For instance, in elder abuse there seems to be greater influence from pathology and less from external stress and history of family violence. The implication of this for policy and programming is that existing elder abuse laws and services should be reevaluated for their appropriateness to the targeted population. For example, Ohio's Protective Services Law for Adults should be amended to include service providers in the fields of mental retardation and alcoholism as mandatory reporters, who are not otherwise covered by virture of professional affiliation.

Besides being modeled after child abuse and so often inappropriate because of divergent etiologies, adult protective service laws and programs also have been developed on the assumption that the major causes of elder abuse were those emphasized in the early literature on the subject, e.g., stress and history of family violence (Langley, 1981). It may be that these factors are important in explaining other abuse forms. They, however, are less important in explaining physical abuse. Existing laws and services need to be reevaluated on the basis of this new understanding of the problem as well.

A final implication of the present study is the need to upgrade and expand adult protective services at county departments of human services. In collecting data for this research, I was struck by the commitment of individual adult protective service workers and their sincere willingness to cooperate in the study. Many gave considerable time to identifying subjects and describing case dynamics during qualifying adult offspring interviews. I was also often struck by the large caseloads of many of these workers, up to 70 cases per worker. With so many cases, workers at these agencies were reduced to crisis intervention activities. They rarely had time for proper case assessment, service networking or case recording. It is likely that some qualifying adult offspring were overlooked by workers as a result. It is also likely that if adult protective services are not improved very soon, a crisis of care will develop of the nature that has occurred in the past with child protective services. As the elderly population grows and the numbers of potential filial caregivers decrease as a result of reduced mortality and fertility, the incidence of elder abuse is likely to increase. County departments of human services mandated by law in Ohio, and elsewhere, to address this problem must be prepared to meet this challenge. Currently, however, there are few initiatives among public officials to facilitate that preparation either through funding or stated concern.

LIMITATIONS OF THE RESEARCH

The present study offers important information on the etiology of elder abuse by adult offspring. It suggests some explanations for abuse occurrence and a sequence for predicting the event. The study is, however, limited in some respects. First, its design lacked a comparison group. Therefore, it is impossible to know, for example, to what extent vulnerability of the elder parent is characteristic of an abuse situation or simply a caregiving situation. Second, the study did not explore certain areas of the proposed conceptual framework, such as ageism. As a consequence, their meaning in explaining elder abuse remains unknown. Third, the research sample was based on referral source record or caseworker recall. Therefore, it probably only included those cases of physical abuse which were recent, memorable or severe. This sample bias limits the generalizability of findings from the study. Fourth, the study restricted its focus to physical abuse by adult offspring. It did not explore other forms of abuse, such as psychological abuse, or abuse by other persons, such as aged spouses. The etiology of these other abuse forms and abuse by other perpetrators may be different than those uncovered through this study. Fifth, the present study limited its inquiry to abuse perpetrators known to hospitals and human service agencies. As a result, its findings are not generalizable to elder abuse among filial caregivers who have not come to the attention of authorities or service providers.

IMPLICATIONS FOR FURTHER RESEARCH

As stated elsewhere, the present study lays the groundwork for research on elder abuse using more rigorous research designs. It suggests hypotheses which may be tested. It challenges some well-established ideas and leaves unanswered questions which indicate avenues for further research. For example, it challenges the emphasis usually placed on external stress as an explanation for elder abuse. It will be important to duplicate the present study to validate this finding.

In addition, the study heightens the controversy over the role of vulnerability on the part of the elder for abuse occurrence. Both early and recent research on elder abuse vary around the importance of this factor, which needs to be clarified if the problem is to be adequately understood and addressed.

Finally, a number of questions arise from the findings of the present study. Future research should attempt to answer them. The questions include the following: Are there other subcultures, besides Appalachia, which promote elder abuse through social acceptance of violence against elders? Are caregivers with certain pathologies more prone toward abuse? How important is the role of financial dependence or greed in abuse infliction? What is the effect of achieved balance of exchange between elder parent and adult offspring in preventing elder abuse? Why are so many abuse perpetrators unmarried, unemployed or unconnected to formal networks or activities? What implications do these characteristics have for abuse occurrence? Is the etiology of other abuse forms similar to that for physical abuse? Is the etiology for abuse by filial caregivers similar to that by aged spouses?

BIBLIOGRAPHY

Achenbaum, W. A.: *Shades of Gray: Old Age, American Values, and Federal Policies since 1920*. Boston, Little, Brown, 1983.

Adorno, T. W., Frenkel-Brunswick, E., Levinson, D. J., and Sanford, R. N.: *The Authoritarian Personality*. New York, Harper & Row, 1950.

Appley, M. H., and Trumbull, R.: On the concept of psychological stress. In Appley, M. H., and Trumbull, R. (Eds.): *Psychological Stress: Issues in Research*. New York, Appleton-Century-Crofts, 1967, pp. 1-13.

Anastasio, C. J.: *Elder Abuse: Identification and Acute Care Intervention*. Paper presented at the National Conference on Abuse of Older Persons, Boston, 1981.

Baines, E.: Caregiver stress in the elder adult. *Journal of Community Health Nursing, 1,*257-263, 1984.

Bandura, A.: *Aggression: A Social Learning Analysis*. Englewood Cliffs, Prentice-Hall, 1973.

Baumhover, L. A., and Meherg, J. D.: *Intergenerational Helping Patterns: Who Cares?* Paper presented at the 35th annual meeting of the Gerontological Society of America, Boston, 1982.

Benjamin Rose Institute: *Family Assessment of Caregiving to Seniors (FACTS)*. Cleveland, Author, 1980.

Benjamin Rose Institute: The effects on families of caring for impaired elderly in residence. *Bulletin*, 1-2, 1982, Summer.

Blau, P.: Social exchange. In Sills, D. L. (Ed.): *International Encyclopedia of the Social Sciences*. New York, Macmillan, 1968, vol. 7, pp. 452-458.

Blenkner, M., Bloom, M., Wasser, E., and Nielson, M.: Protective services for older people: Findings from the Benjamin Rose Institute Study. *Social Casework, 52*(8), 1971.

Block, M. R., and Sinnott, J. D. (Eds.): *The Battered Elder Syndrome: An Exploratory Study*. College Park, University of Maryland, Center on Aging, 1979.

Blumberg, M. L.: Psychopathology of the abusing parent. *American Journal of Psychopathology, 28*(1),21-29, 1974.

Branch, L. G., and Jette, A.: Elder's use of informal long-term care assistance. *The Gerontologist, 23,*51-56, 1983.

Briley, M.: Battered parents. *Dynamic Years*, 24-27, 1979, January-February.

Brody, E. M.: *Long-term Care of Older People: A Practical Guide*. New York, Human Sciences, 1977.

Brody, E. M.: Older people, their families and social welfare. *The Social Welfare Forum, 1981.* New York, Columbia University, 1982, pp. 75-99.

Brody, S. J., Poulshock, S. W., and Masciocchi, C. F.: The family caring unit: A major consideration in the long-term support system. *The Gerontologist, 18,*556-561, 1978.

Brown, J. A.: Combatting the roots of family violence. *Journal of Social Welfare, 6*(2),17-24, 1979-1980.

Burgess, R. L.: Child abuse: A social interactional analysis. In Lakey, B. B., and Kazdin, A. E. (Eds.): *Advances in Clinical Child Psychology.* New York, Plenum, 1979.

Butler, R. N.: *Why Survive? Being Old in America.* New York, Harper & Row, 1975.

Butler, R. N., and Lewis, M. I.: *Aging and Mental Health: Positive Psychosocial Approaches.* St. Louis, Mosby, 1973.

Cantor, M. H.: Life space and the social support system of the inner city elderly of New York. *The Gerontologist, 15,*23-27, 1975.

Cantor, M. H.: Strain among caregivers: A study of experience in the United States. *The Gerontologist, 23,*597-604, 1983.

Caplan, G.: *Support Systems and Community Mental Health: Lecture on Concept Development.* New York, Behavioral, 1974.

Carroll, J. C.: *A Cultural Consistency Theory of Family Violence in Mexican-American and Jewish Subcultures.* Paper presented at the annual meeting of the National Council on Family Relations, 1975.

Chen, P. N., Bell, S. L., Dolinsky, D. L., Doyle, J., and Dunn, M.: Elderly abuse in domestic settings: A pilot study. *Journal of Gerontological Social Work, 4*(1),3-17, 1981.

Cicirelli, V. G.: *Helping Elderly Parents: The Role of Adult Children.* Boston, Auburn, 1981.

Cicirelli, V. G.: Adult children and their elderly parents. In Brubaker, T. H. (Ed.): *Family Relationships in Later Life.* Beverly Hills, Sage, 1983, pp. 31-46.

Cobb, S.: Social support as a moderator of life stress. *Psychosomatic Medicine, 38,*300-314, 1976.

Cobb, S.: Social support and health through the life course. In McCubbin, H. I., Cauble, A. E., and Patterson, J. M. (Eds.): *Family Stress, Coping and Social Support.* Springfield, Thomas, 1982, pp. 189-199.

Comptroller General of the United States: *The Well-being of Older People in Cleveland, Ohio* (Publication No. HCD-77-70). Washington, U.S. General Accounting Office, 1977.

D'Augelli, A.: Social support networks in mental health. In Whittaker, J. K., and Garbarino, J. (Eds.): *Social Support Networks: Informal Helping in the Human Services.* New York, Aldine, 1983, pp. 71-106.

Davies, R., Gallagher, D., Benedict, A., Lovett, S., Priddy, M., and Silver, D.: *Caregiver Burden, Tasks and Experiences.* Paper presented at the 38th annual meeting of the Gerontological Society of America, New Orleans, 1985.

Dentan, R. K.: *The Semai: A Nonviolent People of Malaya.* New York, Holt, Rinehart & Winston, 1968.

Dohrenwend, B. P.: Problems in defining and sampling the relevant population of stressful life events. In Dohrenwend, B. S., and Dohrenwend, B. P. (Eds.): *Stressful Life Events*. New York, Wiley, 1974, pp. 275-310.

Douglass, R. L., Hickey, T., and Noel, C.: *A Study of Maltreatment of the Elderly and Other Vulnerable Adults*. Ann Arbor, University of Michigan, Institute of Gerontology, 1980.

Dowd, J. J.: Aging as exchange: A preface to theory. *Journal of Gerontology, 30,*584-594, 1975.

Edwards, J. N., and Brauburger, M. B.: Exchange and parent-youth conflict. *Journal of Marriage and the Family, 35,*101-107, 1973.

Eggert, G., Granger, C., Morris, R., and Pendleton, S.: Caring for the patient with long-term disability. *Geriatrics, 22,*102-114, 1977.

Environmental factors precipitate abuse. *Journal of Gerontological Nursing, 10*(8),41, 1984.

Fagan, J. A., Stewart, D. K., and Hansen, K. V.: Violent men or violent husbands? Background factors and situational correlates. In Finkelhor, D., Gelles, R. J., Hotaling, G. T., and Straus, M. A. (Eds.): *The Dark Side of Families: Current Family Violence Research*. Beverly Hills, Sage, 1983, pp. 49-67.

Farmer, R. E., Monahan, L. H., and Hekeler, R. W.: *Stress Management for Human Services*. Beverly Hills, Sage, 1984.

Faulk, M.: Men who assault their wives. *Medicine, Science and the Law,* 180-183, 1974.

Finkelhor, D.: Common features of family abuse. In Finkelhor, D., Gelles, R. J., Hotaling, G. T., and Straus, M. A. (Eds.): *The Dark Side of Families: Current Family Violence Research*. Beverly Hills, Sage, 1983, pp. 17-28.

Foy, F. A., and Avato, R. M.: *Catholic Almanac*. Huntington, Our Sunday Visitor, 1968.

Freedman, M., Webster, H., and Sanford, N.,: A study of authoritarianism and psychopathology. *Journal of Psychology, 41,*315-322, 1956.

Friedrich, W. N., and Boriskin, J. A.: The role of the child in abuse: A review of the literature. *American Journal of Orthopsychiatry, 46,*580-590, 1976.

Fuchs, V. R.: *How We Live: An Economic Perspective on Americans from Birth to Death*. Cambridge, Harvard, 1983.

Fumich, J., and Poulshock, S. W.: Stress Provoking Tasks in Family Caregiving Situations. Paper presented at the 34th annual meeting of the Gerontological Society of America, Toronto, 1981.

Garbarino, J.: A preliminary study of some ecological correlates of child abuse: The impact of socioeconomic stress on mothers. *Child Development, 47,*178-185, 1976.

Garbarino, J.: The human ecology of child maltreatment: A conceptual model for research. *Journal of Marriage and the Family, 39,*721-735, 1977.

Garbarino, J., and Gilliam, G.: *Understanding Abusive Families*. Lexington, Heath, 1980.

Gelles, R. J.: *The Violent Home*. Beverly Hills, Sage, 1972.

Gelles, R. J.: Child abuse as psychopathology: A sociological critique and reformulation. In Steinmetz, S. K., and Straus, M. A. (Eds.): *Violence in the Family*. New York, Dodd, Mead, 1974, pp. 190-204.

Gelles, R. J.: An exchange/social control theory. In Finkelhor, D., Gelles, R. J., Hotaling, G. T., and Straus, M. A. (Eds.): *The Dark Side of Families: Current Family Violence Research.* Beverly Hills, Sage, 1983, pp. 151-165.

Gelles, R. J., and Straus, M. A.: Determinants of violence in the family: Toward a theoretical integration. In Burr, W., Hill, R., Nye, F. I., and Reiss, I. (Eds.): *Contemporary Theories about the Family.* New York, Free Press, 1979, pp. 549-581.

Gerstein, J. C., Langner, T. S., Eisenberg, J. G., and Orzek, L.: Child behavior and life events: Undesirable change or change per se. In Dohrenwend, B. S., and Dohrenwend, B. P. (Eds.): *Stressful Life Events: Their Nature and Effects.* New York, Wiley, 1974, pp. 159-170.

Gil, D. G.: *Violence Against Children: Physical Child Abuse in the United States.* Cambridge, Harvard University, 1970.

Gil, D. G.: *A Holistic Perspective on Child Abuse and Its Prevention.* Paper presented for the National Institute of Child Health and Human Development, Washington, 1974.

Gil, D. G.: *Child Abuse and Violence.* New York, AMS, 1979.

Gilbert, N., and Specht, H.: *Dimensions of Social Welfare Policy.* Englewood Cliffs, Prentice-Hall, 1974.

Goode, W. J.: Force and violence in the family. *Journal of Marriage and the Family, 33,*624-636, 1971.

Gottlieb, B. H.: The role of individual and social support in preventing child maltreatment. In Garbarino, J., Stocking, H., and Associates (Eds.): *Protecting Children from Abuse and Neglect.* San Francisco, Jossey-Bass, 1980, pp. 37-60.

Greenblatt, M., Becerra, R. M., and Serafetinides, M. D.: Social networks and mental health: An overview. *American Journal of Psychiatry, 139,*977-984, 1982.

Harrington, J.: Violence: A clinical viewpoint. *British Medical Journal, 1,*228-231, 1972.

Harris, L., and Associates: *The Myth and Reality of Aging in America.* Washington, National Council on the Aging, 1975.

Helfer, R. M.: The etiology of child abuse. *Pediatrics, 51,* (3, Supplement), 777-779, 1973.

Henderson, S.: The social network, support and neurosis: The function of attachment in adult life. *British Journal of Psychiatry, 131,*185-191, 1977.

Hennan, C. B., and Photiades, J.: The rural Appalachian low-income males: Changing role in a changing family. *The Family Coordinator, 28,*608-615, 1979.

Herrenkohl, R. C., and Herrenkohl, E. C.: Some antecedents and developmental consequences of child maltreatment. *New Directions for Child Development, 11,*57-76, 1981.

Hickey, T.: *Neglect and Abuse of the Elderly: Implications of a Developmental Model for Research and Intervention.* Unpublished manuscript, Ann Arbor, University of Michigan, School of Public Health, 1979.

Hill, R.: *Families Under Stress.* New York, Harper & Row, 1949.

Hill, R.: Generic features of families under stress. *Social Casework, 39,*139-150, 1958.

Holmes, T. H., and Rahe, R. H.: The social readjustment rating scale. *Journal of Psychosomatic Research, 11,*213-218, 1976.

Holmes, T. H., and Masuda, M.: Life change and illness susceptibility. In Dohrenwend, B. S., and Dohrenwend, B. P. (Eds.): *Stressful Life Events: Their Nature and Effects.* New York, Wiley, 1974, pp. 45-72.

Homans, G.: *Social Behavior: Its Elementary Forms.* New York, Harcourt, Brace & World, 1961.

Horowitz, A., and Shindelman, L. W.: *Reciprocity and Affection: Past Influences on Current Caregiving.* Paper presented at the 34th annual meeting of the Gerontological Society of America, Toronto, 1981.

Horowitz, G., and Estes, C.: *Protective Services for the Aged* (DHEW Publication No. 74-20101). Washington, U.S. Department of Health, Education, and Welfare, 1971.

House, J. S.: *Work Stress and Social Support.* Reading, Addison-Wesley, 1981.

Hunter, R. S., Kletrom, N., Kraybill, E. N., and Loda, F.: Antecedents of child abuse and neglect in premature infants: A prospective study in a newborn intensive care unit. *Pediatrics, 61,*629-635, 1978.

Hurst, M. W., Jenkins, C. D., and Rose, R. M.: The assessment of life change stress: A comparative and methodological inquiry. *Psychosomatic Medicine, 40,*126-141, 1978.

Jacobs, M., and Dentel, N.: *Elderly Abuse in the Toledo Area: A Report of the Elderly Abuse Task Force.* Unpublished manuscript, Family and Child Abuse Prevention Center and Information Services for the Elderly, Toledo, 1984.

Johnson, B., and Morse, H. A.: Injured children and their parents. *Children, 15,*147-152, 1968.

Johnson, J. H., and Sarason, I. G.: Moderator variables in life stress research. In Sarason, I. G., and Spielberger, C. D. (Eds.): *Stress and Anxiety.* Washington, Hemisphere, 1979, vol. 6, pp. 151-167.

Jones, M.: *Beyond the Therapeutic Community: Social Learning and Social Psychiatry.* New Haven, Yale, 1968.

Justice, B., and Justice, R.: *The Abusing Family.* New York, Human Sciences, 1979.

Kaplan, B. H., Cassel, J. G., and Gore, S.: Social support and health. *Medical Care, 25,*(5, Supplement),47-58, 1977.

Kempe, C. H., Silverman, F. N., Steele, B. B., Droegemueller, N., and Silver, H. K.: The battered-child syndrome. *Journal of the American Medical Association, 181,*17-24, 1962.

King, N.: Exploitation and abuse of older family members: An overview of the problem. *Response, 6*(2),1-5, 1983.

Kirscht, J. P., and Dillehay, R. C.: *Dimensions of Authoritarianism: A Review of Research and Theory.* Lexington, University of Kentucky, 1967.

Kosberg, J. I.: *Family Conflict and Abuse of the Elderly: Theoretical and Methodological Issues.* Paper presented at the 32nd annual meeting of the Gerontological Society of America, Washington, 1979.

Kosberg, J. I.: *Family Maltreatment: Explanations and Interventions.* Paper presented at the 33rd annual meeting of the Gerontological Society of America, San Diego, 1980.

Kunkin, D., and Byrne, M.: *Appalachians in Cleveland.* Cleveland, Cleveland State University, Institute of Urban Studies, 1972.

Langley, A.: *Abuse of the Elderly* (Human Services Monograph No. 27). Washington, U.S. Department of Health and Human Services, Project SHARE, 1981.

Lau, E. E., and Kosberg, J. I.: Abuse of the elderly by informal care providers. *Aging,* 10-15, 1979, October.

Liebert, R., and Baron, R.: Some immediate effects of televised violence on children's behavior. *Developmental Psychology, 6,*469-475, 1972.

Lowenthal, M. F.: *Lives in Distress.* New York, Basic, 1964.

Lundberg, U., Theorell, T., and Lind, E.: Life changes and myocardial infarction: Individual differences in life change scaling. *Journal of Psychosomatic Research, 19,*27-32, 1975.

Maden, M. F., and Wrench, D. F.: Significant findings in child abuse research. *Victimology, 2*(2),196-224, 1977.

Makosky, V. P.: Sources of stress: Events or conditions. In Bell, D. (Ed.): *Lives in Stress: Women and Depression.* Beverly Hills, Sage, 1982, pp. 35-53.

McLaughlin, J. S., Nickell, J. P., and Gill, J.: *An Epidemiological Investigation of Elderly Abuse in Southern Maine and New Hampshire 1979-1980.* Unpublished manuscript, Boston University, School of Nursing, 1980.

Mechanic, D.: Some problems in developing a social psychology of adaptation to stress. In McGrath, J. E. (Ed.): *Social and Psychological Factors in Stress.* New York, Holt, Rinehart & Winston, 1970, pp. 104-123.

Mechanic, D.: Stress and social adaptation. In Selye, H. (Ed.): *Selye's Guide to Stress Research.* New York, Van Nostrand Reinhold, 1983, vol. 2, pp. 118-133.

Miller, D. A.: The "sandwich" generation: Adult children of the aging. *Social Work, 26,*419-423, 1981.

Monahan, J.: *Predicting Violent Behavior: An Assessment of Clinical Techniques.* Beverly Hills, Sage, 1981.

Mueller, D. P.: Social networks: A promising direction for research on the relationship of the social environment to psychiatric disorder. *Social Science and Medicine, 14A,*147-161, 1980.

Nowak, C. A., and Brice, G. C.: *A Review of Familial Support Systems in Later Life: Implications for Mental Health and Social Service Providers.* Unpublished manuscript, Center for the Study of Aging, State University of New York at Buffalo, 1983.

Ohio Bureau of Employment Services: *Ohio at Work: 1984 Chartbook.* Columbus, Author, 1985.

Ohio Data User's Center: *Population by County.* Columbus, Ohio Department of Development, 1985.

O'Malley, H., Segars, H., Perez, R., Mitchell, V., and Knuepfel, G. M.: *Elder Abuse in Massachusetts: A Survey of Professionals and Para-professionals.* Boston, Legal Research and Services for the Elderly, 1979.

O'Malley, T. A., O'Malley, H. C., Everitt, D. E., and Sarson, D.: Categories of family-mediated abuse and neglect of elderly persons. *Journal of the American Geriatrics Society, 32,*362-369, 1984.

Ory, M. G.: The burden of care: A familial perspective. *Generations, 10*(1), 14-18, 1985.

Palmore, E.: Total change of institutionalization among the aged. *The Gerontologist, 16,*504-507, 1976.

Pap, M. S. (Ed.): *Ethnic Communities of Cleveland: A Reference Work.* Cleveland, John Carroll University, 1973.

Paykel, E. S.: Life stress and psychiatric disorder: Applications of the clinical approach. In Dohrenwend, B. S., and Dohrenwend, B. P. (Eds.): *Stressful Life Events: Their Nature and Effects.* New York, Wiley, 1974, pp. 135-149.

Paykel, E. S., and Tanner, J.: Life events, depressive relapse and maintenance treatment. *Psychological Medicine, 6,*481-485, 1976.

Pedrick-Cornell, C., and Gelles, R. J.: Elder abuse: The status of current knowledge. *Family Relations, 31,*457-465, 1982.

Perrotta, P.: The experience of caring for an elderly family member (Doctoral dissertation, State University of New York at Buffalo, 1983). *Dissertation Abstracts International,* 1984.

Phillips, L. R.: Abuse and neglect of the frail elderly at home: An exploration of theoretical relationships. *Journal of Advanced Nursing, 8,*379-392, 1983.

Pillemer, K.: Social isolation and elder abuse. *Response,* 2-4, 1985, Fall.

Poulshock, S. W., and Deimling, G. T.: Families caring for elders in residence: Issues in the measurement of burden. *Journal of Gerontology, 39,*230-239, 1984.

Rankin, E. D., and Pinkston, E. M.: *Family Caregivers and Burden: A Developmental Perspective.* Paper presented at the 38th annual meeting of the Gerontological Society of America, New Orleans, 1985.

Rathbone-McCuan, E.: *Intergenerational Family Violence and Neglect: The Aged as Victims of Reactivated and Reverse Neglect.* Paper presented at the XIth International Congress of Gerontology, Tokyo, 1978.

Rathbone-McCuan, E.: Elderly victims of family violence and neglect. *Social Casework, 61,*292-304, 1980.

Rathbone-McCuan, E., and Hashimi, J.: *Isolated Elders: Health and Social Intervention.* Rockville, Aspen, 1981.

Ray, J. J.: Authoritarianism, dominance and assertiveness. *Journal of Personality Assessment, 45,*390-397, 1981.

Reece, D., Waltz, T., and Hageboeck, H.: Intergenerational care providers of non-institutionalized frail elderly: Characteristics and consequences. *Journal of Gerontological Social Work, 5,*21-34, 1983.

Reynolds, E., and Stanton, S.: Elderly abuse in a hospital: A nursing perspective. In Kosberg, J. I. (Ed.): *Abuse and Maltreatment of the Elderly: Causes and Interventions.* Boston, Wright, 1983, pp. 391-403.

Riddell, F. S.: *Appalachia: Its People, Heritage, and Problems.* Dubuque, Kendall/Hunt, 1974.

Runyon, R. P., and Haber, A.: *Fundamentals of Behavioral Statistics.* Reading, 1977.

Sainsbury, P., and Grad de Alarcon, J.: The psychiatrist and the geriatric patient: The effects of community care on the family of the geriatric patient. *Journal of Geriatric Psychiatry, 1,*23-41, 1970.

Sanchez-Dirks, R.: Reflections on family violence. *Alcohol, Health and Research World, 4*(1),12-16, 1979.

Sangl, J.: The family support system of the elderly. In Vogel, R. J., and Palmer, H. C. (Eds.): *Long-term Care: Perspectives from Research and Demonstrations.* Rockville, Aspen, 1985, pp. 307-336.

Schmidt, M. G.: Failing parents, aging children. *Journal of Gerontological Social Work, 2,*259-268, 1980.

Schorr, A.: *". . .thy father & thy mother. . ." A Second Look at Filial Responsibility and Family Policy* (SSA Publication No. 13-11953). Washington, U.S. Government Printing Office, 1980.

Sengstock, M. C., and Liang, J.: *Identifying and Characterizing Elder Abuse.* Detroit, Wayne State University, Institute of Gerontology, 1982.

Sengstock, M. C., Barrett, S., and Graham, R.: *Abused Elders: Victims of Villains or of Circumstances?* Paper presented at the 35th annual meeting of the Gerontological Society of America, Boston, 1982.

Shainess, N.: *Psychological aspects of wife-beating. Birmingham Post,* 1975, July 12.

Shanas, E.: The family as a social support system in old age. *The Gerontologist, 19,*169-174, 1979.

Simos, G. B.: Adult children and their aging parents. *Social Work, 18,*23-25, 1973.

Soldo, B. J., and Myllyluoma, J.: Caregivers who live with dependent elderly. *The Gerontologist, 23,*605-611, 1983.

Solomon, T.: History and demography of child abuse. *Pediatrics, 51,*(4, Supplement),775-776, 1973.

Spitzer, R. L., Endicott, J., Fleiss, J. L., and Cohen, J.: The psychiatric status schedule: A technique for evaluating psychopathology and impairment in role functioning. *Archives of General Psychiatry, 23,* 41-55, 1970.

Springer, D., and Brubaker, T. H.: *Family Caregivers and Dependent Elderly: Minimizing Stress and Maximizing Independence.* Beverly Hills, Sage, 1984.

Steele, B. F., and Pollock, C. B.: A psychiatric study of parents who abuse infants and small children. In Helfer, R. E., and Kempe, C. H. (Eds.): *The Battered Child.* Chicago, University of Chicago, 1974, pp. 89-134.

Steinmetz, S. K.: *Overlooked Aspects of Family Violence: Battered Husbands, Battered Siblings, and Battered Elderly.* Testimony presented to the U.S. House Committee on Science and Technology, Washington, 1978.

Steinmetz, S. K.: Elder abuse. *Aging,* 6-10, 1981, January-February.

Steinmetz, S. K., and Amsden, D. J.: Dependent elders, family stress, and abuse. In Brubaker, T. H. (Ed.): *Family Relationships in Later Life.* Beverly Hills, Sage, 1983, pp. 173-192.

Steur, J., and Austin, E.: Family abuse of the elderly. *Journal of the Geriatrics Society, 28,*372-375, 1980.

Straus, M. A.: Cultural and social organization influences on violence between family members. *Social Science Information, 12,*105-125, 1973.

Straus, M. A.: Stress and physical child abuse. *Child Abuse and Neglect, 4,*75-88, 1980a.

Straus, M. A.: Stress and child abuse. In Kempe, C. H., and Helfer, R. E. (Eds.): *The Battered Child,* 3rd ed. Chicago, University of Chicago, 1980b.

Straus, M. A., Gelles, R. J., and Steinmetz, S. K.: *Behind Closed Doors: Violence in the American Family.* Garden City, Anchor, 1980.

Sussman, M.: The family life of old people. In Binstock, R. H., and Shanas, E. (Eds.): *Handbook of Aging and the Social Sciences.* New York, Van Nostrand Reinhold, 1976, pp. 415-449.

Thomas, W. R.: The expectation gap and the stereotype of a stereotype. *The Gerontologist, 21,*402-407, 1981.

Troll, L. E., and Nowak, C. A.: How old are you? The question of age bias in counseling adults. *The Counseling Psychologist, 6,*41-43, 1976.

U.S. Bureau of the Census: *General Population Characteristics: Ohio.* Washington, U.S. Department of Commerce, 1981.

U.S. House Select Committee on Aging: *Elder Abuse (An Examination of a Hidden Problem)* (Committee Publication No. 97-277). Washington, U.S. Government Printing Office, 1981.

U.S. House Select Committee on Aging: *Elder Abuse: A National Disgrace* (Committee Publication No. 99-502). Washington, U.S. Government Printing Office, 1985.

U.S. Senate Special Committee on Aging and U.S. House Select Committee on Aging: *Elder Abuse: Joint Hearing.* Washington, U.S. Government Printing Office, 1980, July 11.

U.S. Senate Special Committee on Aging and American Association of Retired Persons: *Aging America: Trends and Projections.* Washington, 1984.

U.S. Senate Special Committee on Aging: *How Elder Americans Live: An Analysis of Census Data* (Serial No. 99-D). Washington, 1985.

Villmoare, E., and Bergman, J. (Eds.): *Elder Abuse and Neglect: A Guide for Practitioners and Policy Makers.* San Francisco, National Paralegal Institute, 1981.

Vinakur, A., and Selzer, M. L.: Desirable versus undesirable life events: Their relationship to stress and mental distress. *Journal of Personality and Social Psychology, 32,*329-337, 1975.

Walker, L. E.: *The Battered Woman.* New York, Harper & Row, 1979.

Walker, L. E.: The battered woman syndrome study. In Finkelhor, D., Gelles, R. J., Hotaling, G. T., and Straus, M. A. (Eds.): *The Dark Side of Families: Current Family Violence Research.* Beverly Hills, Sage, 1983, pp. 31-48.

Weller, J. R.: *Yesterday's People.* Lexington, University of Kentucky, 1965.

Wilcox, B.: Social support in adjusting to marital disruption: A network analysis. In Gottlieb, B. (Ed.): *Social Networks and Social Support.* Beverly Hills, Sage, 1981.

Wilensky, H. L., and Lebeaux, C. N.: Conceptions of social welfare. In Weinberger, P. E. (Ed.): *Perspectives on Social Welfare: An Introductory Anthology.* New York, Macmillan, 1974, pp. 23-30.

Williams, J. H.: *Psychology of Women: Behavior in a Biosocial Context.* New York, Norton, 1977.

Wolf, R. S., Godkin, M. A., and Pillemer, K. A.: *Elder Abuse and Neglect: Final Report from Three Model Projects.* Worcester, University of Massachusetts Medical Center, University Center on Aging, 1984.

Wood, V., and Mueller, J.: Self-maintenance and community behavior of adult retardes. In Schreider, M. (Ed.): *Social Work and Mental Retardation.* New York, Day, 1970, pp. 701-714.

Zalba, S.: Battered children. *Transaction, 8,*58-61, 1971, July-August.

Zald, M. N.: Introduction. In Zald, M. N. (Ed.): *Social Welfare Institutions: A Sociological Reader.* New York, Wiley, 1965, pp. 1-10.

Zarit, S. H., Reeves, K. E., and Bach-Peterson, J.: Relatives of the impaired elderly: Correlates of feelings of burden. *The Gerontologist, 20,*649-655, 1980.

NAME INDEX

A

Achenbaum, W. A., 9, 113
Adorno, T. W., 87, 113
Amsden, D. J., 7, 8, 13, 120
Anastasio, C. J., 5, 113
Anetzberger, G. J., v, x
Appley, M. H., 11, 113
Austin, E., 4, 5, 15, 120
Avato, R. M., 62, 115

B

Bach-Peterson, J., 121
Baines, E., 12, 113
Bandura, A., 9, 113
Baron, R., 8, 118
Barrett, S., 120
Baumhover, L. A., 12, 113
Becerra, R. M., 116
Bell, S. L., 114
Benedict, A., 114
Bergman, J., 6, 121
Blau, P., 16, 113
Blenkner, M., 3, 113
Block, M. R., 4, 6, 7, 9, 15, 17, 58, 62, 113
Bloom, M., 113
Blumberg, M. L., 10, 15, 113
Boriskin, J. A., 15, 115
Branch, L. G., 12, 113
Brauburger, M. B., 16, 115
Brice, G. C., 4, 118
Briley, M., 9, 113
Brody, E. M., 4, 12, 113, 114
Brody, S. J., 12, 114
Brown, J. A., 13, 114
Brubaker, T. H., 12, 52, 120
Burgess, R. L., 15, 114

Butler, R. N., 3, 9, 114
Byrne, M., 91, 117

C

Cantor, M. H., 12, 114
Caplan, G., 14, 114
Carroll, J. C., 62, 114
Cassel, J. G., 117
Chapman, V., ix
Chen, P. N., 6, 7, 9, 10, 13, 14, 15, 58, 114
Cicirelli, V. G., 12, 114
Cobb, S., 14, 114
Cohen, J., 120
Coulton, C., ix

D

D'Augelli, A., 14, 114
Davies, R., 12, 114
Deimling, G. T., 12, 119
Dentan, R. K., 19, 114
Dentel, N., 5, 117
Dillehay, R. C., 87, 117
Dohrenwend, B. P. 11, 115
Dolinsky, D. L., 114
Douglass, R. L., 6, 7, 9, 10, 13, 15, 115
Dowd, J. J., 16, 115
Doyle, J., 114
Droegemueller, N., 117
Dunkle, R., ix
Dunn, M., 114

E

Eckert, K., ix, 40
Edwards, J. N., 16, 115
Eggert, G., 12, 115

123

SUBJECT INDEX

A

Abuse, 29, 57, 67, 68, 90, 93
  definition, 28
  incidents, 36, 57, 58, 74-75
  measurement, 44-45
  recent, 39, 57, 74-76
  risk indicators, 106
  types, 36, 57, 58, 74, 104-105
  verification criteria; 33
Abuse occurrence, steps triggering (*see* Stress, acute)
"Abuse of Elder Parents in the Home" research project, ix, 40
Abuse-prone personality (*see* Personality, abuse-prone)
Abuse socialization (*see also* Family violence, history of), 8-9, 17, 19, 21, 22, 23, 26, 27, 28, 29, 31, 62, 72-74, 94, 104
Adult offspring, definition of, 28
Adult protective services, 4, 25, 56, 109
Adult protective services laws, 5, 25, 33, 108-109
Age, vii, 36, 45, 56, 57, 58, 59, 61, 71, 96, 104
Ageism, 6, 9, 19, 22, 23-24, 27, 28, 94, 95, 110
Alcoholism (*see also* Pathology), 6, 10, 11, 23, 25, 29, 46, 57, 63, 80, 94, 105
Alcoholism service system, 107-108, 109
American Association of Retired Persons, 4, 59, 121
Antielder attitudes (*see* Ageism)
Appalachian culture, x, 42, 53-54, 75, 91-93, 95-96, 101, 104
Appropriateness for interview, 35, 36, 38, 103
Ashtabula County, 31

B

Battered old person syndrome, 3
Battered parent, 3
Battered women (*see* Spouse abuse)
Behavioral response, abuse as a, 21-22
Benjamin Rose Institute, 12, 32, 113
Burden of Elder Caregiving Index, 48, 66

C

Caregiver stress (*see* Stress, internal)
Caregiving (*see* Elder caregiving)
Case analysis, 5, 6
Case Western Reserve University, ix, 40
Catholic (*see also* Religion), 51, 61, 62, 104
Child abuse, 3, 4, 6, 9, 10, 13, 15, 17, 18, 29, 38, 72-73, 95, 108-109
Child discipline, 49, 53, 72, 74, 92, 105, 108
Chronbach's alpha, 47, 48, 52
Cleveland, 12, 32, 42, 108
Cleveland Mediation Program, 32
Cleveland Metropolitan General Hospital, 32
Coding, 45, 55
Comptroller General of the United States, 12, 114
Conflict tactics, vii, 72-76, 105
Conflict Tactics Scale, 49-50, 72, 74
  Violence Scale, 45, 49, 54, 58, 72, 92
Consent to cooperate, 34-35
Construct validity, 99

Assistance (*see* Help received)
Authoritarian personality (*see* Personality, authoritarian)
Authoritarians, The, 87-89
Availability for interview, 35, 36, 38, 103